BACKWARDS IN TIME

BACKWARDS IN TIME

A Study in Infant Observation
by the Method of Esther Bick

ALESSANDRA PIONTELLI

Clunie Press
for
The Roland Harris Trust Library
Monograph No. 1

Typeset by Ace Filmsetting Ltd, Frome
Produced by Radavian Press, Reading

Contents

To the memory of Esther Bick

Preface

When Esther Bick introduced her method of infant-mother observation into the training of child psycho-therapists at the inception of the course at the Tavistock Clinic in 1948 no one foresaw the immense impact and influence it was to accrue over the years. Gradually it became the keystone of that training in observation and thought about children as the groundwork upon which therapeutic techniques needed to be founded. It spread to the Institute of Psycho-analysis and then to training systems in France, Italy, Norway, Spain, Australia, and South and North America as the former students of the Tavistock Clinic carried it abroad. The emphasis that Mrs Bick placed on detailed observation and reporting to the discussion group of each student's weekly observations helped to keep interpretive impulses at bay so that the language of observation naturally remained unburdened by jargon, but rather tended towards the poetic.

But restraint in the interpretation of mechanisms and meanings was not intended to restrain intuitive recognition of emotional participation and identificatory processes, in keeping with the growing use of the observation of counter-transference in psycho-analytical technique. A talented display of this method is to be found in Dr Piontelli's accounts of Martin and Jack.

Perhaps even more surprising than the rapid establishment of this method as a training technique was the gradual emergence of its research value. I can well remember, not without some shame, my own early scepticism about Mrs Bick's enthusiasm in this direction. I did not realise how the serial observations would allow for the emergence of patterns which were invisible among the plethora of events in the single observations, especially the earliest ones. But slowly the insights gained from this method began to make compelling links with the data from psycho-analytic therapy with psychotic children. Certainly it played a part in the work reported in *Explorations in Autism* and in the more recent paper on non-autistic states reported at the Monaco meeting in 1984 and contained in *Studies in Extended Metapsychology* (Clunie Press, 1986).

I remember the impact made on the seminars in Perugia in 1978 when Dr Piontelli reported on Martin's development; never have I seen a group so moved, almost shattered by a clinical report. The reader will soon discover the reason which lies not only in the material but in the vivid and passionate way in which it is recorded. Like the case of Sara reported by Dottoressa Anna Sabatini Scolmati of Rome, which was contained in our Monaco paper, Martin represents the features both of a Failure of Post-natal Mental Adjustment, and of a Primary Failure of Mental Development, both non-autistic forms of infantile psychosis. The failure to achieve an object relationship which could foster symbol formation (Bion's alpha-function) is brilliantly illustrated, along with a catalogue of the phenomena of adhesive identificatory processes which proliferate in the absence of such a projection-introjection interchange.

Jack, on the other hand, presents a child of a probably somewhat more vigorous constitution growing in a non-environment but with other severe defects. Perhaps the fact of his being a boy after the parents had had three girls, perhaps the change in their economic circumstances which permitted the mother to stay at home, perhaps the relative absence of the father, perhaps these and other factors all combined to alter the atmosphere of the mother-child relationship from what it had been in the case of the other children. At all events Mrs T comes through as somehow emotionally 'burnt out', an absent mentality, warm but unthinking. Mrs T's inability to be worried, even in the later stages of the observation period, must reflect her earlier inaccessibility to the child's non-verbal communications. The resultant process of progressive withdrawal is heart-rending, though less enraging to the reader than is the account of Martin's malignant environment. Strangely the results are very similar in the two children and present us with a puzzle which shows up the inadequacy of our model for understanding the early stages of personality development.

While studies of a more or less purely descriptive sort like this present one may seem to move our understanding very little forward by themselves, they do emphasise the importance of this field of research. The problem of keeping observation relatively free of the preconceptions which our technical language has built into it is clearly illustrated, for in the case of observation of babies in particular, we are thrown back on the emotional responses in ourselves by which we intuit the baby's experience. The practice of psychoanalysis, with its great requirement of sensitivity to the countertransference, would seem to be the training ground for such work. But by this same token the record of these observations may seem too subjective and 'unobjective' to readers not experienced in this field of work. But thus are all languages fundamentally untranslatable.

Donald Meltzer

Introduction

In this small book I would like to describe my experience of two infant observations. The difference between them will become apparent as I proceed with my description. The social and economic backgrounds of the two families could not have been more diverse. In the first I was moving in a wealthy upper-class Anglo-French family whereas in the second I went to the outskirts of London to a poor, gloomy working-class area. The characters of the various members of the two families were also quite distinct and the two babies, on the whole, were developing very differently. Yet in spite of these factors I was more and more struck by many similarities in the development, or rather non-development, of both babies, and this was my main reason for deciding to select, put together and compare these two among the many babies which I had observed.

The observations were upsetting experiences for me; they felt almost unbearable at times, yet I learnt a lot through them. They led me to look at other situations in a different way as I gradually realised that the phenomena I was observing were much more common and widespread than I had originally believed. Nevertheless, I hope that my account will read as an interesting 'story' and place these sad events in a constructive perspective. Each observation follows a course of several years, and the first one in particular now has the benefit of many years' hindsight.

In each case I start by describing my initial contact with the two mothers and then go on to describe the other members of the families. After that I try to trace the development of each situation and, in particular, of each baby as I was able to observe it. Through reasons of space I report only a few observations in detail and my description is done mainly through my retrospective account of them. At the end of the book I try to review the two observations and to draw some general conclusions. These are by no means theories for, if anything, I was left with more questions than answers, but they are tentative attempts at an explanation of some of the phenomena I observed in these particular babies which might be described as a regressive move ·backwards in time to an illusory womb-like state. In my review I focus mainly on the earlier part of these children's development, both because I was able to observe it more closely and because I think that in infant observations one has the unique opportunity of seeing, almost at birth, hints of the means and mechanisms one will meet in later pathology as well as normality.

In the bibliography I refer only to the main theoretical background which accompanied me at the time and which helped me to give more meaning to my observations in retrospect. This is not because I consider these theories to be marginal. Indeed I believe them to be so central that I hope that the reader will either already know them, and therefore be able to recognise them between the lines, or will want to read them directly and not just through my shadowy, second-hand version of them.

In addition to books and theories two people were by my side almost throughout these observations: Mrs Martha Harris during the first, and Mrs Esther Bick, particularly during the first year of the second. Without them, their teachings and their support this book could not have seen the light. Yet ultimately all the responsibility for what I say in this book, including its confusions, mistakes and short-comings, remains mine only.

I

Martin

[I observed Martin regularly for about two and a half years. Then my visits continued on a more or less yearly basis. Martin is now eleven years old.]

Mrs T[1]

I first met Mrs T in November, 1971. She was introduced to me by Dr S who was my gynaecologist at the time. I was looking for a mother to observe and I asked him whether he could help me to find a suitable one among his patients. He phoned a few days later to say that Mrs T had immediately accepted the idea of an observer coming regularly to visit her and that the baby was due in about a fortnight. He told me that she was very wealthy, living in Belgravia and he described her as an intelligent woman, modern, full of life and with wide interests, although he also added that she was living a rather confused life, probably not what one would expect to be an ideal mother to observe but certainly an interesting person. He also told me that she was in her late thirties, married to a French nobleman who had just recently settled in England. She already had a daughter of two from a previous marriage or perhaps a former boy friend. Dr S did not know what her profession was, but he thought that she was involved in some kind of artistic activity; nor did he know what her husband's profession was, but since he was wealthy, he probably lived on his family fortune. He did know that he was mad about sailing, gambling and polo.

I did not question Dr S further about what he meant by Mrs T's confused life, although it did sound as if the situation was not going to be an easy one to observe. I decided to contact Mrs T all the same. When I rang her for an appointment she immediately bombarded me with questions. She asked me my age and my child's age; she said that she knew that he had been born by Caesarean section as Dr S had told her this. She asked if I was planning to have another child soon, and she also said that she knew that I was a doctor. She asked some more

[1] This observation is an enlarged, revised edition of a previous paper presented in October, 1979 in Perugia at a seminar on autism. It was subsequently published in 'Quaderni di psicoterapia infantile', vol. 3, Edizioni Borla, Rome, under the title 'Tra Bi-dimensionalità ed Autismo'.

details about my profession, such as where I was working, when I had started, if it was far away, etc. She also asked me what my husband's profession was. This inquisition poured out almost non-stop. She asked many more questions and I remember feeling irritated by her interrogation and also found it somewhat intrusive. I felt a little annoyed with Dr S for giving her so much information about me despite my careful explanations that this was undesirable. We arranged for an appointment for the following week, about ten days before the baby was due.

When I went to visit her in her huge Belgravia flat Mrs T's appearance immediately struck me. (This meeting took place in 1971 when punk rockers were almost unknown.) Though it was only 3 p.m. she was dressed in a very long, low-cut black velvet dress and she was wearing very high heels and a strange pair of black knee-length socks. She was not very tall, rather slim, her hair was dyed, her make-up was strange, with lips painted black, and she wore a lot of heavy jewellery. Apart from black being the dominant colour, her clothes, make-up, accessories, etc. seemed curiously ill-assorted, consisting of strangely juxtaposed and ill-digested items found in the latest fashion magazines, an inharmonious mixture of the macabre and the sexy. Her pregnancy was very evident, yet this too was quite at odds with the rest of her ensemble.

As she moved she looked worldly and theatrical, as if she were going to perform in front of a large audience. Her 'stage' the huge and grandiose drawing room with its heavy, long, tightly drawn, dark velvet curtains making it impossible to distinguish night from day, together with the ornate period furniture and the numerous antiques, all accorded well with her appearance. Hanging on every possible wall was an incredible collection of wooden, marble and bronze lifesize *putti*, looking in the darkness of the room like a macabre display of dead and petrified babies who had never seen the light of day.

After the first formal greetings she seated herself in a theatrical fashion while constantly playing with her hair, hands, necklaces, and again started to talk, once more bombarding me with questions more or less the same as those she had asked over the phone. Her eyes were unfocused and she did not seem to be listening to my answers. Then the subject of her talk turned to herself. The first thing that she told me was that she was going to have a Caesarean as she had done on the occasion of her daughter's birth. But apart from that everything else was to be different now as she had a new husband. He too had been married before. It had all been a mess and a confusion. But the confusion was in her almost continuous talk which provided me with disjointed bits and pieces of the most varied kind of information, much of which was impossible to piece together in a coherent whole.

She then returned to the subject of the Caesarean. She said she had both wanted and chosen to have one for she was quite terrified of labour with its unbearable pain and terrible risks. The picture she presented of natural delivery (though again it was a confused and fragmentary one) was of something so awful, nightmarish and dangerous that nobody could possibly survive it, mother and baby could not possibly come out of it alive. Anaesthesia and oblivion were the only possible answers. "With a Caesarean you do not know or realise what's happening . . . everything is easier . . . the child comes out without effort . . . and the mother feels no labour pains . . ." The subsequent description she gave of the pain of a Caesarean section felt on the days following the operation was also of something excruciating and unbearable as if, no matter how it happened, birth could only be a shattering, violent event, a kind of mortal incision or wound. But it was very difficult to detect any emotion in her voice: no matter what the subject was the 'play went on' and her utterance always had the same 'on stage' high-pitched quality; her face wore the same social 'party' expression.

The Caesarean quite soon, in the almost continual flow of her conversation, became a link between us: we had both had one. She appeared to feel that between us there was a total sharing and she took on what she thought was my 'role' and my 'part'. She became an expert in pedagogy, pouring out in confused succession all her theories on child-rearing and education. She then gave me an idealised picture of her daughter and of her relationship with her. Shortly after this her daughter Gloria came in, beautiful and almost solemn in her silence and the intensity of her look. Mrs T for the first time looked anxious and unsure, a little like a beginner in front of a real prima donna. She told me her daughter was admired by everyone for her beauty. Even a famous man like Lord B was madly in love with her and kept her picture on his desk.

It was almost time for me to go and I asked her some questions about her family and work (something I now would not do). She said that she had no brothers or sisters, no memories of her childhood and she made a grimace when I asked about her mother. Then she said, "My mother is terribly anxious . . . while I remember being very calm with Gloria . . . of course it is better if one worries about things . . . I am sure that if I had to leave Gloria with someone I'd leave her with my mother . . ." As to her work, I could hardly follow what she said in the confused outpouring of facts, name-dropping, aspirations, projects, etc. that followed my question. I understood that it had something to do with the theatre but I could not tell if she was an actress, a playwright, a producer, or what. Even now, after so many years of contact with her, I do not think that I quite know what her work was, if indeed she ever had any. During the observation she also told me that she was soon going to move into a much larger flat, just a few blocks away. While accompanying me to the door she told me what the baby's name was going to be. She had not contemplated the possibility of its being a girl; she already had one. Then she added, bursting into laughter, that he was going to be called Martin, like her previous husband as well as her former boy friend.

Throughout this observation I remember at times feeling uneasy, shocked and irritated. In a sense the unease always remained during the years that followed, particularly as I observed poor Martin, so dependent on her if he was to be able to open up to the world, while progressively withdrawing from it. Sometimes it was almost unbearable for me to be merely a powerless and impotent observer of what was happening around and mainly inside him. [In fact in both these observations I did not remain merely a passive and silent witness all along. In Martin's case I told the parents of my disquiet about the way he was developing and suggested professional help. I also reported to them what I had seen of their maid's behaviour. Unfortunately Mrs T did not seem to be able to listen very much to what I had to say; if anything she withdrew even more into her mindless activities. However, my words possibly had an indirect impact on her husband as his attitude changed quite a lot. The role of observer in infant observation would require a long disquisition outside the scope of this book.] As to my irritation and sense of shock regarding Mrs T's appearance, her way of 'acting' and of presenting herself, these quite soon disappeared and were replaced by feelings of sadness and genuine pity which I have retained throughout the years whenever in contact with her.

I soon realised that behind her sexy, modern (in the sense of in-the-latest-fashion), ostentatiously wealthy and worldly façade there was something extremely fragile, almost non-existent about her, like a tiny germ that needed all the glitter it could gather to survive the complexities of life and to carry on at least with a surface existence. Under the surface she was, and felt, like a tiny, very fragile and not-yet-ready-to-be-born primitive and undifferentiated creature. I also came to feel more and more that in a sense such a creature had never seen the light, had never come out of its sheltering cocoon or experienced a proper 'psychological birth'. In fact she seemed to deploy all her resources and energies to prevent such a birth happening, busy as she was in trying to recreate for her tiny germ-of-a-self a quasi-womb-like seclusion, a quasi-physical, tight muscular wrapping. In fact in the very first meeting she had told me this clearly with her nightmarish description of birth and her wish to be unconscious of it in spite of her terror of anaesthetics. She also said later (see Observation One), "You know, I hate anaesthetics. You know, I hate things getting out of control . . . that is why I don't drink . . ." But the alternatives were only, as I have said, unbearable pain and death.

Later on, on a few occasions, she literally poured out all her fears about being "out". As she told me several years later, during one of my then occasional visits to her family (see Observation One), "You know, I also went to see a neurologist . . . you know, I always have this terror of going out . . . and last summer I really felt ill . . . I was at the seaside. . . . I was terrified of going out . . . also I was crying all the time just for no reason . . . and I was feeling sleepy all the tme as well . . . you know, I couldn't even go out of the house . . . or take a bus . . . or anything". Later on she added, "Even now I find it difficult to go out. I can only stay in a familiar place . . . I even find it difficult going out shopping . . ." Another time she told me about feeling empty, with no strength at all, unable to do anything or to perform even the simplest tasks. She also felt terrified "of falling to pieces", of feeling faint, and in a sweat whenever confronted with too many people or with unfamiliar surroundings. She felt, I think, like a tiny, weak, utterly parasitic creature unable to survive on its own, unable to have an independent life and sufficient individual strength if torn away from the familiar and vital wrapping of the womb. Nothing else seemed familiar to her, devoid as she was of the experience and memory of opening up to the light of a different scene, or at least of the experience and memory that such an opening was not going to end with a mortal wound or deadly severance.

But apart from what Mrs T told me I also observed all this for quite a long time. She would often sleep and then wake up for so-called breakfast or lunch at the most unusual hours of the afternoon, as if she were living in a separate world with little distinction between sleeping and waking life, and in a time dimension totally independent of what went on outside, what other people did, the passage of time, varia-tions in temperature and light, etc. The curtains of her drawing-room and of her equally huge bedroom were always closely drawn and I often had the oppressive feeling, when visiting her, of entering a huge, dark, often silent, crypt-like princely tomb. I remember that I always emerged from her flat with a feeling of great relief, as if suddenly breathing and seeing the light again. [Exposure to aerial respiration, changes in temperature and light, and to varied sounds and the appearance of other people, wider scenes, and so on together with a progressive reduction in sleep as well as a proper differentiation between sleeping and waking-time are, of course, all characteristics to be met in life after birth.] When not asleep she would be engaged almost non-stop in lots of different, all equally purposeless activities. She would move about aimlessly in her flat, though always seeming compelled by some urgent necessity. She would also go out, usually just to the hairdresser, to the park or to the few smart shops round the corner (even Harrods was too far away for her), again making these expeditions sound like vital and imperative ones. She would spend hours engaged in obsessive, mindless activities, like brushing her hair or making up her eyes. She would also receive visits from many of her so-called friends, a strange collection of the most unusual types that came and went like shooting stars, leaving, I believe, no trace behind them after the initial 'jet-settish' sparkle. But beyond this apparent physical and social movement, the overall feeling was that her life was something extremely narrow, empty and constricted within the tight boundaries and confined limits of her 'safe', golden cocoon (after all, even foetuses move quite a lot inside the womb). Many of her bodily and mental resources were used also to create a womb-like protection for herself; for instance by talking all the time, almost non-stop, during the observations. She would often choose a subject, any subject, and then go on proliferating in a more and more mechanical and repetitive way. It was difficult to piece together any deeper link or thread in her talking, as what she was saying did not seem to have a real core. Her phrases, like her words, seemed to be joined more through contiguity of sound or surface meaning than through any deeper link or continuity. Just to quote an example from the first observation, she told me at one point, "My cousin . . . what a mess. She is never with her children . . . but at least three children . . ."; it was mainly the sound of the word "child" that led to the next topic or question. I could quote many such observations.

The same applied to her way of reasoning. For instance, in the first observation she told me that everything was different and new this time: she had a different husband, and she was going to have a new baby, a new flat was also needed, quite soon she would have a new maid and a whole set of different clothes, etc. When something was new then everything else had to be new. Just the sound of the word "new" – a physical, superficial quality – seemed to be the main link underlying this chain of apparently consequential thoughts. She also used clichés, empty bits of fashionable jargon picked up here and there and put together, often oddly assembled, without any coherence and meaning – like the unhomogeneous mixture of her fashionable clothes. Her continuous talking did not seem to have the quality of communicating. It was more a physical, mechanical, almost muscular activity to 'keep going', to keep herself together and to wrap round herself a tight impenetrable membrane of familiar words. Her movements, like her excitement and the 'talking activity', all seemed to provide her with armour. Filled up and entirely occupied by this she seemed quite untouched and unaware of anything else in the world. Also when 'pouring out' her fears (which happened very rarely) the feeling was more of a discharge or of an evacuation, again something muscular or excretory rather than a proper projection or communication with a human and mental recipient. [All this again reminded me very much of the condition of a foetus, who, having not met with mental 'recipients', clearly cannot use mental communication with them and therefore can only resort to such physical expressions as evacuation, discharge, etc. At that stage communication can perhaps take place through physical contact or through a particular receptivity and sensitivity to even slight physical changes. But proper projection is probably quite alien to that stage: you might say that you can only project if you have a space and a place into which you can project.]

She spent most of her talking time on the phone. Quite often while breast feeding Martin she would pick up the receiver and start phoning at random until the feed was over. Later when the bottle or even when the spoon was introduced, after a couple of minutes she would call in the maid and ask her to continue the feed as she had to go out or make some urgent phone call. She would spend hours in what sounded to me like endless monologues holding the receiver (I often doubted if anyone was there listening) as if it were simply an apparatus which she was using, rather than that she was talking to a live recipient who could answer back in a non-predictable, non-mechanical way. In fact she did not seem to be wanting or expecting any answer or any to and fro conversation or discussion. She also behaved similarly with me. After the initial shock of her bombardment of questions during our first contact by phone, I soon realised that her questioning had little intrusive or inquisitive purpose. It had more the quality of keeping any other knowledge at bay, as if this latter could only be felt like an intrusion or a bombardment or a breach into her well-known, well-explored cocoon. I realise now, looking back at my notes, how my questions or remarks felt to her like a potential threat. Usually she would not listen to my answers or take in my questions at all: she would for instance ask me something and then stare into space as if my answer had not penetrated her shell. Or else she would pick up what I had said or asked, at least some of it, and proliferate and expand on it with so many other words that in the end it all became part of her; it became part of her 'system'; the stimulus and the source were totally neutralised and obliterated. At other times she would just want to know some small item, usually an already well-known piece of information, that was just enough to put me in a well-defined place inside the narrow limits of her mental territory.

Equally she would look for superficial similarities in people and erase any differences between them. For instance, the similarity with me was our common gynaecologist or the fact that we had both had a Caesarean. But I think that she was frightened of finding out any deeper similarity or any difference. Once she had found a superficial contact she stuck to that and all the rest was obliterated. She somehow stretched to the utmost the point of contact and flattened out all the differences, moulding the other person around herself, till only a flat, shadowy and distorted outline remained. She also moulded herself around the idea of other people, acting like them. But because of the way she perceived others, her acting always sounded like a rather pathetic, partial, often wired performance as for instance in the first observation when she became an expert in pedagogy. For her, I think, all this represented the illusion of an undivided, total contact, of an almost physical, perpetual link. Any deeper contact, any deeper perception or any deeper link with people (including me) was felt as something frightening, as a terrible intrusion and a threat to that sort of illusion. Any proper and sustained scrutiny, like any proper and sustained contact, would inevitably reveal the differences and complexities of another personality. This contact, like her eye contact, usually never lasted more than a few seconds. Very often, as I said before, while talking to me or while feeding the baby, her eyes seemed to be out of focus. Either she would stare vacantly, miles away, or else she would look fixedly at her 'familiar' hands, at her hair, at her necklaces and rings, and play with them almost non-stop, constantly keeping herself company with them.

Needless to say her relationship with her husband, like her relationship with her children, with other people and with me, appeared to be very superficial. She seemed to need a quick, almost physical contact with people, a quick and physical sparkle. The contact, as I said before, was established at once. She immediately accepted me as an observer and she seemed excited at the prospect. A link was formed, almost physically, through sparkling excitement, but this link would rarely last for more than a second. She would, for instance, frequently go into Martin's room, pick him up, tickle and joggle him up and down, kiss him and then quickly move on to something else, to another source of excitement, leaving him mostly in the care of her maid. Anyone or anything would do, provided it gave her the spark. Then in a second she would move to another source of 'sparkling light', a bit like the attraction of insects and moths to any source of light at night.

She often presented a frank sexy image of herself, through the clothes she wore, or her behaviour with her friends, or in her choice of friends, and so on. Again I had the impression that in all these manifestations there was a superficial kind of excitement. She seemed to need excitement to build up a 'skin', to build up an external surface. This excitement also gave her a sort of pseudo-life to fill up the emptiness behind the surface and therefore prevent its collapse. This same excitement also seemed to obliterate any separation, any skin boundaries. Through it she achieved a kind of fusion or illusory total union with whomever happened to be there at the time. She would often treat Martin like an exciting object, like a penis, manipulating, massaging and stimulating his body. She would spend hours absent-mindedly playing with his actual penis quite forgetful of the fact that she only intended to clean it.

Most of the time she seemed to need something concrete, like a real child or a possession in order to fill up what to me seemed more and more like a desperately felt, utterly empty space inside her; her collection of precious objects, of antiques, and particularly of the carved wooden angels and *putti*, those wooden, immobile, concrete babies, increased to an amazing extent so that soon her rooms became crowded with them, hanging on every possible surface. At the same time the number of real babies in her family began to increase rapidly, especially if we consider that she had four in only a few years. Had it not been for a still birth and the danger posed by too many Caesareans I am sure that their number would have increased even further. But once the baby was out, living autonomously, or even when it began showing some autonomy by beginning to move inside her womb, she lost interest in it and quickly made plans for the next one.

External values too seemed all important to her. Money, status and, once the baby was born, observable and measurable facts such as its weight, its smiles, held great significance for her and provided her with a security that she did not possess in herself. Without such external measures she seemed quite lost, possessing, I believe, no steady identity or orientation. In a sense one could never tell where she was, or where she really stood in relation to herself. Frantically busy following the latest flash of light or holding onto the most fashionably accepted values, she never seemed firmly contained inside her skin. Most of the time she gave the impression of living inside someone else's skin or womb. Even her body, with its autonomous, uncontrollable movement often felt like something alien to her: heart beats, intestinal movements, periodic flows – all could be felt at times like mysterious forces coming from another 'foreign body' that persecuted and threatened to annihilate her almost non-existent self. As she once told me, "My body is no longer my own . . . it's like living inside someone else's or having someone else living inside me . . ." Given the primitiveness of her mental state, her thinking too still seemed very much anchored to her body, with its concreteness, its reflexive, almost muscular quality, its flat predictable movement and monotonous repetitive flow. She seemed to live most of the time in a kind of 'sensation-based' or 'impulse-dominated' primitive world, just following the sensation of the moment and responding almost automatically to it, which resulted in total lack of memory not only of her childhood, but of the most recent past. ountless times, after having just told me on the phone that I could come and visit her immediately as she was free, I was told on arrival that she had just gone out to the hairdresser, or was sleeping, or was busy with a friend – and the expression of sincere, total surprise on her face when eventually she saw me testified, I think, to her innocence of intent to mislead.

Mr T

I met Mrs T's husband during the second observation when I went to visit her in hospital a few days after the delivery. Our first meeting certainly was not an easy one. I would never have expected in an infant observation to have to defend myself against the father and two of his friends, but they immediately launched an 'attack', trying to seduce me in the coarsest 'Latin-lover' style.

The three men were obviously waiting for me, with one already acting as a *pappagallo* as soon as he spotted me in the main corridor of the maternity ward. At first I thought he might have been a new father who had lost his head under the emotional stress, but soon the real nature of the plot became too grossly obvious. Consequently my first impression of Mr T was not a favourable one. In appearance he was somewhat strongly built, with a dark complexion, longish dark hair and mandarin-style moustaches; he was wearing a black pin-striped suit, pointed, rather high-heeled patent leather shoes and an unbuttoned shirt, with a heavy gold medallion dangling on his hairy chest. With his strong French accent to top it all, he reminded me more of a character from a twenties gangster film than of a typical 'good' father.

During this same observation it became quite clear that he had formed a kind of 'homosexual gang' with his two friends whose purpose was to attack, mock and destroy women in general and the infant-mother couple in particular. Being a woman, and clearly being interested in the couple, I also was attacked and mocked by them. Mr T's only reply to my asking about the baby was "he is really ugly", accompanied by loud laughter. I could read from his expression his firm belief that my 'real' interest lay in something quite different; they all 'knew' it could not be in the mother-baby couple but must be in their own 'irresistible virility'.

The room was full of flowers and Mrs T was looking very tired, terribly pale and obviously in great pain though unable to rest or to stop her aimless wandering around. No one was showing her any sympathy, busy as they all were in their 'exciting' activity of cruelly teasing and mocking her. Later, during the observation, she showed me a huge pile of pornographic comics and magazines. She told me that her husband had brought them there so that she could "read them during the confinement". Prostitution, necrophilia and sadism were prominent in the titles, as well as being depicted on the brightly-coloured covers; women were illustrated as prostitutes or as being sadistically attacked, torn to pieces and lacerated like hunks of meat.

When I became the direct target of their 'seductive' efforts, my first reaction was to flee, wondering how on earth it had come about that when only seeking, if not a 'holy', at least an ordinary specimen of a so-called 'normal' maternity, I had instead landed in the middle of an orgy. But then I decided to stay and to try to be firm, though always ready to run in case this had no effect. To my surprise my firmness caused the almost immediate flight of the three men who quickly left the room, a little like children caught in the middle of some clandestine, naughty activity by the sudden arrival of an adult. In all this Mrs T certainly was at least a silent accomplice. But my feeling was that she derived some kind of initial excitement and then went along with them rather passively and with decreasing conviction, just unable to put a stop to their behaviour. In fact she seemed rather relieved when the three men left, as if the game had really gone too far. She could then talk about the Caesarean and the baby, and complain about her sufferings and exhaustion.

As for me, it took a while to recover from the initial shock but, as I have related, my firmness did seem to have made some impact on Mr T and, thinking it over in retrospect, I am the more convinced that in the long run I won his respect. However, for quite a long time, whenever I met Mr T he seemed to treat me as someone to be held in utter contempt. At best I was a servant and the moment I walked in he dumped the baby in my arms saying, "Oh, here she comes . . . now at last we can get rid of him . . . you can look after him for a while . . ." But most of the time he would try to form an alliance with his wife or with whomever happened to be present, joking and laughing excitedly and hinting at shared 'secret' topics. The aim of all this was to try to make me feel like a pathetically poor creature, excluded from their wonderfully exciting sexuality and from his gracious and powerful virility which he kept 'dangling' in front of me. With all the others (including quite often Gloria) he could behave with perfect and exquisite gallantry, like a Prince Charming, or an expert and gracious Don Juan. I was the only one who, out of stupidity and inexperience, simply could not understand. He would quite often drop phrases like, "she is poor . . ." or "she doesn't understand . . ." but always indirectly, while talking to someone else, as if I, "poor thing", wasn't even worthy of direct attention. But unfortunately someone else, poor little Martin, was also treated with similar mockery and contempt; his father used to laugh at him and say he was ugly, pathetic, fat and stupid; he laughed at his smallness and at his many obvious inabilities, including his undeveloped sexual capacities. In this he could always readily find an ally in other members of the family. And undoubtedly Gloria was chief among these. Whenever Martin looked at his father, or later smiled or stretched out his arms towards him, laughter was the only response he elicited. Most of the time he met with no response at all as his father was usually busy directing his attention towards more important and exciting people.

Yet gradually Mr T's attitude towards me began to change and, in parallel, his attitude towards Martin seemed to alter. He began to show genuine appreciation of my continued interest in his child and his family. He would now greet me as a friend and behave in a kind, mostly non-seductive way; he would see that I was offered a chair and a drink and he would also tell me briefly what Martin had been doing and what his impressions of him were. But most important of all, his attitude towards Martin (who was now about ten months old) began to change. Not that the picture became an entirely rosy one. For instance, he would sometimes treat Martin seductively, in a lover-like way, kissing him sensuously on erogenous zones, such as his lips, his neck, behind his ears, while whispering things like, "You are driving me mad . . ." or "Look what you have done to me . . ." etc. He also began to show increasing irritation and, I think, competition towards his wife, frequently criticising her behaviour towards the children with phrases like, "You see, she is like that . . . three minutes a day she bounces him up and down, kisses him and that is all . . . she has fulfilled her duty . . .", or "If it had been up to her we could all have died within a very short time . . . she doesn't even care about our survival . . . I am only able to win through because I deserve the Nobel Prize for patience and goodness . . ." But their relationship continued to survive and the sexual atmosphere between them was always there whenever I saw them together. The number of Mrs T's pregnancies testified moreover that it was something more than just an atmosphere.

Yet, as I said before, beyond all this Mr T also began to show a genuine interest in and concern for Martin's difficulties and behaviour. He would now sympathise with him and call him "my poor little thing" without any laughter or mockery, showing tenderness, affection and, at least unconsciously, real sadness about Martin's increasing poverty of feelings and emotions. He would pay him more than three minutes' attention and, on a couple of occasions, I actually saw him playing with Martin (and Gloria) for the entire length of the observation. I am sure that this was not done just to show me what a good father he could be. Not surprisingly Martin became very attached to him. "Daddy" was the first word he said and Daddy was the first, if not the only person whose presence he acknowledged and whose absence he intensely noticed. This was the situation, at least up to the time when I stopped visiting his family regularly. Martin was then about two and a half years old. After that I only saw him occasionally and never again with his father so it is difficult to know what subsequently went on between them. During my visits I could only observe how Martin's attitude towards people in general was progressively hardening, but I do not know whether this also applied to his father.

A few years later, when Martin was about seven years old (see Observation One), Mrs T told me one day of some nightmarish events that had happened since we had last met. She told me how, during the summer, her husband had almost died of a haemorrhage. He was well and fully recovered then but he had been in hospital for a long time. The uncertainty had been terrible and he had undergone a very complicated and risky operation. For the first time, on that occasion, Mrs T also expressed some real anxiety about Martin's development. She told me, amongst other things, that Martin had shown no reaction at all to his father's illness: "He didn't show any distress or anything . . . but he was saying his rosary all the time . . . you know he picked up this habit from a Spanish maid." Saying his rosary had by now become one of Martin's favourite obsessive activities which he would often retreat into. But I think from what I was able to observe that it was at least partly due to his father's changed attitude that Martin's retreat from the world did not in the end become total.

Gloria

Martin's elder sister was three and a half at the time of his birth. Gloria was a bit like her name, beautiful and 'superior', above everyone and everything. For her, Martin was so "small" and "utterly despicable" that he did not seem to exist. Later on he became her pale shadow and her slave and regarded her as his undisputed Queen, and as such she naturally treated him with contempt and could only look down on him.

She also felt, and in one sense was, superior to her mother: she was much less fragile and un-integrated and much more determined and conscious of what she did and wanted. It was impossible to ignore her good looks and her piercing and determined way of looking at people. And if a look had not been enough you certainly could not ignore her piercing and determined screams with which she imperiously commanded, and usually instantly got, whatever she wanted. Her attacks against Martin were certainly quite conscious and immediately reached the target, achieving their object with great accuracy. She knew what would frighten him most: for instance, loud noises or too close a physical contact, and whenever she could she turned the television on full volume or tightly clasped him in her arms in what might have looked like a hug but for him was a suffocating, vice-like, terrifying grip. She almost instinctively knew how to torment him, choosing the most suitable 'torture' for each occasion. Just to quote a few examples: by violently shaking his cot; scratching him; pushing him; snatching food and objects out of his hands; calling him stupid when he succeeded at anything. Most tormenting were her frequent interference and intrusions whenever he was receiving any attention, especially from his mother. She would then ask urgent 'metaphysical' questions, 'discuss' interesting topics, make funny remarks, till in the end she attracted all her mother's attention (which was slight anyway) and he was completely abandoned. All this was done with great nonchalance and apparent indifference. One perceived in her mostly hostility rather than terror. Her mother often seemed intimidated by her and frequently placated her. She would treat her as an adult and an equal, giving her complete freedom of choice. She would share with her sexy jokes and funny remarks about Martin and would always take her with her to the hairdresser. She also seemed to admire her capacity to excite admiration, attract compliments and even obtain valuable presents. For Mrs T all this represented a kind of status symbol, a safety anchor; for Gloria it was simply triumph. In relation to Martin it was again triumph – as she used to say, "He is ugly; I am beautiful . . ."

In fact he was rather ugly, fat and shapeless, with small eyes, somewhat coarse features and a sweaty, spotty complexion. All his mother's attempts to launch him into the world of "beautiful people" failed miserably: nobody looked at him. Gloria's superior position was once again assured.

Gloria hated any possibility of change, particularly since her unique position had been threatened by her brother's arrival, an event certainly not planned and decided by her. All the articles in her room (and possibly in the house too) had to remain in the identical position which she had chosen. But behind her rigid and meticulous control I felt there was (if compared with her brother or mother for instance) much less fear, much less terror of disintegration should her rigid boundaries be broken or changed. With her it was more the exercise of power and cruel control over other people, over her objects, whom she could see and recognise from the outside and whom she paralysed and rendered powerless and small inside. Apart from her mother, her sphere of influence and power seemed to extend to other members of the family as well. As I said before, Martin soon became her shadow and, as soon as he could walk, he literally became her follower.

Her grandparents (Mrs T's parents, particularly the father) were mad about Gloria and treated her like their 'real', ideal daughter; she would often spend week-ends and holidays with them, and come back with presents which she displayed and dropped around the house with great nonchalance so that the others, 'the poor', could be aware of the extent of her riches. Her grandparents also often visited and phoned her, almost totally ignoring the rest of the 'progeny', including their real daughter who, indeed, was often rebuked for not treating Gloria with due regard and consideration.

Gloria also had considerable influence on her stepfather, Mr T, who clearly treated her like a woman rather than as a child. The seductiveness of their games was unmistakeable and Gloria frequently won his attention, coaxing him away from her mother. She was in fact quite convincing in her role of the 'woman', a much better actress than her simple-minded mother. She sounded much less convincing in Martin's role, in the role of the baby, which she only rarely took on and dropped almost immediately because of the laughter her performance elicited from the audience.

Gloria soon realised that I was not seduced by her tricks. On a few occasions, while engaged in more or less secret masturbation, she actually caught my glance and from the way she responded to it I also knew that 'she knew I knew'. Her first reaction had been to try to form an alliance with me: since we both belonged to the superior race of those who knew (all the others were too naïve, stupid or poor) we might as well laugh at them and join forces. But she quickly realised that I wasn't going to be drawn into this alliance and thenceforth treated me like a servant: as on the occasions when, in an imperious tone, she asked me to pull up her knickers. In a few instances she took on my own role and would defiantly announce, while pushing me aside, "Now I am going to observe Martin . . . I am the one who looks . . ."

Martin – the first six months

I saw Martin for the first time in hospital when I went to visit Mrs T three days after the delivery. When I arrived he was in the nursery and I have already described how, during the observation, Mrs T continued to move aimlessly and almost non-stop about the room. When I was about to leave she suggested going to see him in the nursery. Martin was quietly sleeping in his cradle and I could not see much of him, but what struck me at the time was the fact that it was I who recognised him from the numberplate on his cradle. Mrs T continued vainly to search for him and could not recognise him at all although he was right under our eyes, the very first baby in the first row. When I pointed him out to her she just said, "But why isn't he moving?" and sounded rather anxious in her own absent-minded way.

I saw him for the second time at home, when he was about fifteen days old. Mrs T was once more particularly restless that day; she was continually moving about, constantly changing from one activity to another, from one one topic to another, without pausing a second. It was quite painful to watch her movements as she looked deathly pale, terribly tired and obviously still in great pain from the after-effect of the Caesarean. Almost each step or movement elicited winces of pain. Martin was sleeping in his cradle, without moving at all. Mrs T made several attempts to wake him up, but with no success. She looked worried as he still failed to move, and she again said, "But why isn't he moving? . . ." and you could read from her expression the absolute conviction that stillness could never mean peace but could only mean death, as if the baby had no 'means' other than his own movements to keep and feel alive. It was only after shaking him rather violently that he began to emerge from sleep.

His first movement was to push out his tongue and to suck it noisily. Then he began to move his head from side to side, rhythmically and without opening his eyes. Mrs T almost immediately put him to the breast. He kept his eyes closed and again I was struck by his complicated and noisy wrapping of the nipple round his tongue, as if he were trying to 'incorporate' it. When she pulled the nipple out of his mouth he again began sucking his tongue and rhythmically moving his head from side to side without opening his eyes, maintaining a continuity as if nothing had happened. When Mrs T put him to the other breast I noticed that, though still sucking, this time he somehow used his tongue to keep the nipple at a distance. Then again as she pulled the nipple out he went on sucking his tongue and moving his head from side to side. During the remainder of the observation he was apparently asleep and he kept almost completely still. Only at one point, when Gloria turned the television on full volume in another room did he seem to react, closing his eyes tightly and plunging his head into his pillow, with an expression of intense, physical pain on his face.

For a long time these all became familiar and constant features of each observation and some of them, later on, familiar and constant elements of his character. Such, for instance, as his difficulty in waking up to a new, different world and to new, different sensations, not merely physical ones, such as being put to the breast. He experienced the impingement of everything (including the nipple) coming from the world – the world we all live in after birth – as a sharp, violent intrusion to be neutralised at all costs and with all available means, in case such impingement would drag him out and shake the stillness of the familiar, solitary world of the womb. He made desperate and vain attempts to plunge back 'in', as if nothing had intervened, and he was able to return to a mindless, hypnotic mental stillness, back to a world of soft rhythmical sounds and of limited, well-tested physical movements (such as those of his head and tongue). He made desperate attempts not to awaken his mind, to keep his body still and his eyes and senses shut away in a state almost of nothingness and of complete suspension of life. It was as if time had stood still before his senses and his mind, as well as the germ of his individual body, had 'woken up' and the unstoppable flow of development and life had been set in uncontrollable motion. He used all kinds of 'hypnotic' means (such as the movement of his head or of his tongue) to plunge himself back into this state of mindless dissolution and suspension of life, or an utterly primitive 'fusion' in which he was neither dead nor yet alive, but just on the borderline between the two.

During the first observations, up until Christmas when he was about two months old, Martin was immobile and apparently asleep most of the time. His stillness seemed like a tense, desperate tightening up and closing of every possible pore. In his complete, stiff immobility he seemed more to be paralysed with terror than peacefully immersed in a blissful, restorative sleep. The few times I saw him open his eyes he was at the breast and he looked up at his mother's face and almost seemed to cling to it with his eyes. His eyes seldom met his mother's and then it was only for a second, not enough to 'hook' or engage him; it was somehow a fixed, almost bewildered look, as if he had dimly and instinctively expected some kind of an unknown yet easily recognisable 'hooking' and 'linkage', and had then been left confused and bewildered, as if in a void. While breast-feeding him Mrs T was usually engaged in non-stop talking in one of her endless telephonic monologues, holding the receiver with one hand, Martin with the other.

The moment she finished feeding him she immediately put him down in his cradle and quickly went out of the room. She seldom spoke to him. Usually she would ask him things like, "Are you happy?" and then immediately break off any contact.

During the Christmas holidays Mrs T moved with her family to a new, even more spacious flat. As the moment of departure drew nearer she seemed to be in a state of complete panic; her constant moving, talking, going out, etc., took on an even more desperate quality. Now that her external 'shell' and 'anchorage', her familiar walls and her familiar environment, were going to be removed and changed she seemed to experience a terrible fear of disintegration. All this reminded me very much of her fears of the birth and of the delivery. Just before I left for the holiday she told me, while shaking my hand, "It's terrible . . . I feel as if I were going to faint . . . or fall to bits . . ." Probably my absence over the holiday was an added element in her panic. Without claiming at all to be of any vital importance in her life, I think that I was already by then at least 'part of the furniture', a steady something that could be expected to be there at a certain time, on a certain day, not much differentiated from a concrete and material object, but perhaps still something.

When I went back to visit her after Christmas, when the move had already taken place, she told me that she had felt terrible during the holiday. She told me about her fears of fainting and "vanishing", of "sweating to death" and "losing all substance". One evening at a party she had been overwhelmed by panic and had briefly lost consciousness once she found herself in the middle of a crowd. The bombardment of stimuli and the changes had really been too much for her. But all this was said in her usual 'pouring out' fashion, as if she was almost physically purging an equally physical experience. Nor do I think that I was especially selected as a good 'container' for her anxieties, for a few minutes later she was pouring out the same 'story' to one of her friends over the telephone.

The maid

Around Christmas time a new maid arrived and she remained with the family until Martin was about two years old. She was rather attractive and I was immediately struck by her silent, almost oblique expression and smile, like that of someone knowing and seeing a lot. In fact she did know and see a lot. Like Gloria she correctly perceived Martin's needs and weak spots, and she certainly did not use her perceptions to help him. Instead she used them as instruments of sadistic pleasure and power. She provoked and teased him, openly laughing at his weakness and at the same time she would stimulate him in all sorts of ways. For instance she immediately noticed things like the importance of his tongue to him and the way in which he filtered everything through it. Later on she noticed the great importance of food and his desperate clinging to it. She seemed to know exactly what his 'addiction' was and used such knowledge to 'hook' him and render him dependent on her. She would often touch his tongue; she would snatch bits of food out of his mouth and then dangle those same titbits in front of his bewildered eyes. She would kiss him on his mouth. She would eat with deliberate, provocative slowness, standing in front of him, consuming whatever he would have liked or expected to eat himself. All this was done silently with a subtle, almost imperceptible smile of excitement and superiority. I cannot help wondering what else went on more or less silently; on a couple of occasions I actually noticed her masturbating while Martin was with her in the same room.

In the meantime her presence silently and progressively infiltrated the family; in the end she almost dominated it. Mrs T placated her with expensive presents and treated her like an equal with pressing familiarity. She tended to imitate or adopt some of the maid's attitudes and would be ready to believe anything she said (including some incredible stories of witchcraft). She and the maid would also join in the exciting activity of laughing together at Martin, or at Mrs T's mother, or at other people or objects. This seemed to give Mrs T a quick spark of life and excitement. Nevertheless the maid's main influence was still over Martin, particularly since Mrs T increasingly left him in her dubious care.

When I came back after Christmas, having missed two observations, I was told that Mrs T had given up breast-feeding almost completely. No reasons were given to me for this. When presented with the bottle I noticed that Martin would immediately arch himself backwards slightly, stiffening up and showing a remarkable muscular control compared with two weeks earlier. He would mostly keep the teat at a distance with his tongue, as if he felt it was a terrible intrusion, but I do not think that it was just the teat that seemed to him like an intrusion. His tongue was 'ever-present'. The moment that he woke up he would suck it and he continued sucking it before, during and after the feed. It seemed to represent the only steady and constant object that he could hold onto while other objects were kept at bay by it.

He gradually began sleeping less during the observations. When awake (but also when asleep) he would mostly keep stiff and still as if even the slightest uncontrolled movement might shake and alter his rigid, yet extremely fragile boundaries and the protection that he was trying to build up for himself through this muscular rigidity and tension. The only exception was his usual rhythmical, constant, monotonous head movement. While moving his head he seemed to be completely filling himself up with his own sensations and movements, creating around himself an impenetrable 'carapace' of 'hypnotic', trance-like insensitivity towards any other sensation coming from the outside. When in such a 'state' Martin did not seem to be hearing, feeling or seeing anything else.

When he was about three months old I began to notice that he was perpetually sweating profusely, especially during his feeds or whenever he looked more than usually tense and rigid; at such times it was possible to see sweat almost streaming out of every pore. (When he was about one month old Mrs T had told me once that he was always in a sweat but I myself had never noticed it before.) When covered with sweat Martin did not seem to possess a protective barrier, a skin, with its natural semi-filtering quality. His rigid, sensuous and muscular barrier seemed in fact a completely 'leaky', non-protective one. Everything could simply leak out, just as everything could get in. People touching him, and sounds in particular, seemed like violent intrusions, like concrete weapons bombarding, invading, and destroying his all too open and vulnerable space. More than once I heard his mother say laughingly to him, "But it's not right inside you, you know . . ." while watching his violent, painful reaction to an unexpected sound. On such occasions he would look terrified. He would also try to cover his ears, close his eyes and withdraw. Then he would immediately resume his obsessive movement and his trance-like expression.

Now that I more frequently saw him awake, it became noticeable that Martin would seldom cry and that when he did he would suddenly scream with terror. It did not seem to make much difference whether he was in someone's arms or in his cot with no one around. His infrequent screams sounded more like evacuations than communications. There did not appear to be any hope that there would be an answer or that these screams would make any impact on anyone. In fact they seemed like sudden, violent expulsions or ejections of some unknown substance into an empty space, very similar to his constant emission of sweat.

When he was about four months old Martin began to increase the range of his rhythmical, constant movements. He would now move his feet up and down, or almost imperceptibly shake his head, particularly when he was given his bottle. But he would also pull up his bib, covering his face and mouth with it and he would vigorously resist if anyone tried to remove this 'shield'. He very seldom made any movement to reach out towards other people. Sometimes he would stretch out his arms to his mother, as if asking to be picked up, but then almost immediately the quality of his movement would change and instead he seemed to be using his arms to ward her off, to keep her at a distance, if not at bay. The same sort of thing happened with his smiles, for around that time, to my great relief, I had begun to notice some smiles. But as soon as he gave the shadow of a smile his tongue would be there. He would then immediately put it out, like some kind of effective plug, or diaphragm, or weapon of defence. For Mrs T smiles were very important fixed 'land-marks'; smiling meant happiness and she would therefore often ask him to smile. Once she had obtained such a smile she would quite happily leave it at that. Martin somehow learned his lesson and did his duty, smiling back quickly in a stereotyped, automatic way, so as to be left alone again as soon as possible to carry on with another of his automatic, endless rhythmical activities.

Martin now gradually began to look around, although usually his look did not travel or explore very far. Almost as soon as he opened his eyes he would find an object and stare at it fixedly and rather blankly. If the object moved out of view (this often happened, for instance with his mother's face), he would frequently continue to stare at the point in space where the object had been before, trying desperately to keep the surrounding scene as fixed and immutable as possible. For this purpose inanimate objects were obviously better, but it did not seem to make much difference in the end whether the object was a person or a thing; his look was always equally blank. In fact he very seldom seemed to ask or express much with his eyes, the only exceptions being terror or bewilderment, particularly if something unexpected happened or whenever he was exposed to too many stimuli (for his low standards), including people entering too often into his fixed orbit.

Around this time I began to notice how he would often scratch his face, violently rub his eyes, cover his ears with his hands, or sometimes jab his fingers into them, sometimes scratching them slightly. As his muscular strength and control increased his face became covered in scratches and I sometimes saw him scratch himself until he bled.

All these activities usually took place in solitude when he was alone in his cot. When he was about five months old I began to notice that these private, self-tormenting activities had taken on an additional quality – excitement. Now whenever he was left alone in his cot he almost immediately abandoned himself to what looked to me like an 'orgy' of sensations, scratching and rubbing his eyes and face, poking his fingers into his ears, all done to the noisy accompaniment of his ever present tongue. They all seemed violent and painful sensations, but his expression was one of intense 'painful pleasure'. The only companion of these solitary orgies was a small sheet, always there in his cot as everyone knew of his attachment to it. He would either take it in his hands and make it a participant in his activities or else, more frequently, he would wrap up his face in it, creating a kind of veil or shield, and all the while he would be moaning with pleasure. The element of excitement made me wonder how much the maid, progressively taking over with her secretive and perverse 'exciting' activities, was beginning to have an impact on him and was becoming part of the images that, willy-nilly, were starting to populate his world. I say 'willy-nilly' because on the whole my impression was that he was increasingly retreating from contact with the outside world, or that at least he was trying desperately not to be open to it.

When intent upon his solitary self-tormenting activities, often veiled with his sheet, he seemed to have gone back to a much more primitive, sensation-based, solitary, mindless world. When in that state he seemed to avoid contact with the outside world; while filling himself with intense physical sensations he became at the same time blind and insensible to what went on around him, as if he were anaesthetised. Yet, in spite of his efforts, the world was obviously beginning to make a strong impact on him. When plunged in his orgies he also seemed to reproduce within himself his private, personal tragedy. The scene was always the same: that of some entity acting as a cruel tormentor and a violent intruder into his self, with little differentiation, perhaps even complete fusion with and confusion between the tormentor and his own tormented self. The kind of representation of the world he seemed to have in mind was that of a solitary place where hopes were cruelly excited, only to be violently crushed, and where pleasure could be derived only by inflicting pain and violating and destroying another's boundaries.

In his world, contact became a violent bombardment or physical intrusion. Nobody was at hand to understand him, to make him feel loved and valuable, worth understanding and therefore able to render his own emotions meaningful and valuable to him – as something that could be felt and thought about, and which did not need violent and immediate rejection or evacuation. In such a world nobody helped the baby to grow, but violence was done to its skin, to its organs of perception, to its self which was not allowed to grow nor helped to develop beyond the world of physical sensation and concrete objects. In this world eroticism replaced warmth and the baby was torment-ingly held or pushed back to live in a mindless, 'hot' animal state. Yet such a state probably felt safer to Martin; at least it was well-known, and he clung desperately and compulsively to it. Outside the covering of the womb he only met with terror, bombardment, blankness, or with humiliation, treated one moment as a mere sexual object, only to be laughed at a minute later because of his obvious smallness and sexual inadequacy.

When he was about five months old it became noticeable how physical pain seemed to have no meaning for him. For instance, on a number of occasions I noticed Gloria scratching him; another time I saw her twisting his wrist (on each occasion, needless to say, I did not remain an observer but actively stopped her). Yet Martin never showed any reaction. As time went on, this characteristic became increasingly evident. Later, when he was beginning to take his first steps, whenever he fell or bumped his head against some sharp edge or corner his only reaction, if any, would be one of surprise. Later still when exploring the house, he was particularly attracted by drawers, but each time he pulled one out (or tried to), he also managed to crush his fingers violently, but again he showed no reaction, not even of surprise, as if 'being crushed' was all that could 'naturally' be expected from exploration beyond one's own closed boundaries. Everyone in the family "knew" he would crush his fingers, but the usual reaction was laughter and mockery; no one taught him to recognise, to become familiar with such pitfalls and therefore be more able to avoid them.

But apart from his being anaesthetised to pain, which he did not seem to know or recognise either mentally or physically, there were many other sensations and emotions which he did not register. To him emotions seemed to be just disturbing 'objects', probably similar to some kind of physical discomfort, something to be rubbed off or scratched away, or to be given off like some secretion through the skin. Potential mental pain did not seem to hurt him but just felt like some particularly strong physical sensation. When something potentially upsetting happened, such as his father laughing at him or Gloria snatching his sheet from out of his hands, he reacted by rubbing his eyes or scratching his hands. Or else he showed no apparent reaction at all although one could see subsequently that he was covered in sweat. His sweating was in fact more and more in evidence; he was often almost dripping wet, especially when being fed. His mother began to notice this (it was impossible to overlook) and that he began to smell unpleasant in spite of his being frequently changed, washed, strewn with talcum powder and sprinkled with eau de cologne. It was certainly not his bodily hygiene that was being neglected.

After each feed he looked tired and strained, never satisfied or contented – these were emotions that he did not seem to know. When someone picked him up or talked to him or smiled at him, his muscular tension and his efforts not to be caught off guard were such that in the end he looked exhausted. When left alone he never seemed peaceful or relaxed, busy as he always was with his private rituals to arouse sensations within his own body, such as shaking his head or sucking his tongue. Whenever he was caught unprepared by an unexpected sound or by one of Gloria's clever moves, and could not avoid awareness of something living autonomously outside him, he seemed intensely frightened and paralysed with fear. It was as if the experience of a change, even for a second, originated by someone or something outside and separate, and the experience of separateness and maybe even of life itself, meant for him something terrible, something much worse than death.

At times he also seemed to lack a sense of continuity and harmony with the autonomous life of his own body. For instance, he would look terrified whenever caught unprepared by some unexpected, uncontrolled movement of his body, such as sneezing, or coughing, or breaking wind. He would then look afraid and bewildered as if the event had been provoked by some dangerous foreign substance inside a body that no longer seemed to belong to him. Immobility and inanimateness seemed to be his only 'ideal' state.

Around the end of the fifth month he began to grasp and cling to objects (an initiative remarkably absent before), but he almost only clung to and grasped inanimate objects at which he would just stare fixedly. He seemed to prefer to hold on to his high chair or to the edge of his cot rather than, say, his mother's neck or arm. Whenever his mother, or any other member of the family, went out of the room he showed no reaction or apparent awareness of this but would turn automatically to some inanimate object, fixedly staring at it while also grasping it. In so doing, everything else and the whole scene seemed to be obliterated from his mind.

The maid had by now become the most fixed presence in Martin's life; he spent hours in her company. During the observations Mrs T was often not present at all, although perhaps phoning or sleeping in her room. Martin seemed to be particularly open to and defenceless against the attacks of the maid. With her he did not even seem to be able to employ his usual defences, such as building walls of muscular activity or barriers of sensory self-stimulation. When she appeared in his line of vision or when he heard her voice or footsteps, he just seemed to lay himself bare and open like an impotent victim offered for sacrifice. With his arms wide stretched, his legs apart, his eyes and mouth also open, no longer looking stiff, but now flaccid and bone-less, he looked like a pathetic skinless creature which had just died after being crucified. He then accepted anything from her.

But apart from this openness to all attacks from the maid, he was at least becoming more physically powerful and less impotent. His body, with its growing complexity of skills and capacities now seemed to come to his aid.

Six months to the first year

When he was about six months old Martin began to sit up. Very soon he was able to stand, and from then on I hardly ever saw him lying or sitting down, at least not of his own free will. If anyone tried to push him down, trying to make him sit (people frequently tried to do this knowing what his reaction would be and laughing at it), he would scream with a mixture of terror and stubborn determination. He certainly seemed determined to become less vulnerable and at other people's mercy. His stronger musculature could now at least give him the illusion of serving this purpose: armed with it he need no longer feel fear and he would be invulnerable to all attacks.

By now he was able to grasp his bottle firmly and to control it. Food took on an ever-increasing importance for him and he became incred-ibly fat. Through overeating, rashes, pimples and spots began to appear. The doctor repeatedly attributed these to indigestion and also found that his liver was considerably enlarged. An appropriate diet was prescribed. However, the maid as usual perceived his addic-tion to food and relentlessly fed it, giving him more and more to eat, with the passive collusion of Mrs T. He would swallow anything without apparently tasting it or discriminating. He seemed con-stantly hungry and was ceaselessly searching for something to ingest. The moment any food was swallowed and was no longer felt by his tongue or mouth he frantically began searching for the next bit. Items were swallowed one after the other giving him relief for a brief moment, but this was never a long-lasting or deeply satisfactory sensation. Inevitably food would leave his mouth just as the nipple had done previously. No gap could be tolerated even for a moment: something else had constantly to be there.

Once swallowed, food became merely a heavy, undigested and unassimilated accumulation – something completely meaningless that could never be fit for digestion and integration at a mental level. It became an intoxication. Even when food was in his hands he could never let it go; he always had to have a firm grip on it. If, for instance, anyone took away his bottle or, later on, his spoon or the piece of banana which he was greedily gulping (both Gloria and the maid were specialists at this), he would immediately look pale, bewildered and paralysed with fear, as if he had been deprived of life itself. Sometimes he would briefly scream, as if in fear and pain, or as if a vital limb had been cruelly and inexplicably amputated, leaving him bleeding to death. On such occasions his ever-present, ever-moving tongue would lie inertly in his mouth and he would dribble from the sides of his equally inert mouth, as if spilling out all his 'substance'.

It usually took him a while to come to life again; the first sign of his recovered vitality was regularly a return to his obsessive ritual movements, such as shaking his head and constantly moving his feet or tongue up and down or round and round. By this means he somehow seemed to wind himself up again, at the same time building a muscular armour and protection whilst also neutralising and absorbing the 'shock' or wound. This he did by building around it a kind of circular web or scar tissue until the occurrence was either rubbed off, or at least closely encapsulated within himself. His tongue was almost always on 'active service' and only very rarely (as on the occcasions which I have described) in a state of inertia. It appeared, somehow, that this was always his best organ of defence, the only one which had stood the longest test of time; after all, it had always been there under his command and control, irremovably and reliably a part of himself; it could be called upon at any moment. One could see it in action mainly in the following ways: he could protrude it and stretch it to push away items like the teat, or he could try to keep them at a distance, at bay and under his control; or he would surround the object (food for example) and apply friction to it, rubbing it in such a way that the foreign body finally became almost 'fused' and assimilated to it, and any difference in taste or texture was effectively rubbed off. Any difference and separation from the object was thus avoided, any gap was closed through 'fusion' and any pain resulting from the difference and separation was neutralised.

His tongue was not only used to repel persecution and pain; in itself it often became an 'object of pleasure', such as during his 'deliciously painful orgies', when in the solitude of his cot he would act out, undisturbed and in complete control, all sorts of perverse, exciting masturbatory relationships and activities with parts of his own body.

His growing bodily strength increasingly came to his aid and, equipped with it, he tried to serve himself. As I have already indicated, by six months he could stand up unsupported. Just before the summer, when he was eight months old, he took his first steps alone. When I came back from the holidays (he was by then nine months old) he was walking alone and his gait was far from unsteady. As the maid once told me, "He moves all the time . . . he gets around everywhere in the house . . . he doesn't want to be picked up or held in anyone's arms . . . he just wants to go around alone . . ." But I think that it was more than just wanting to be on his own. Before the holidays he had begun to show a desperate need for isolation; when he was seven or eight months old everyone, not just strangers, seemed to him to be persecutors. No one could touch him without his reacting with screams of fear, followed in seconds by the persecutor seeming to be right inside him for, while still screaming, he would usually begin to scratch his own face and hands. To him, even his own image seemed to be strange, alien and persecutory; I once saw him standing in front of a long mirror in the corridor screaming, terrified at his own reflection and violently scratching his body.

Before the holidays, when he was about eight months old, I began to notice how his stare would often become glassy and blank. This happened most frequently when other people were around (just around, not directly touching or interfering with him), and whenever he was faced with someone or something which might have the potential of causing him anxiety, one could almost at once see his eyes become unfocused. People were put out of focus and reduced to blank images. His anxiety was similarly unfocused, as it were, and his mind seemed to be reduced to a complete blank as if he had reached some kind of anaesthesia or suspension of mental life. All his other feelings, tastes, likes, etc. seemed just as much out of his field of vision and beyond his recognition. Except when it came to 'raw' emotions like fear, he seemed, at least on the surface, emotionally blank as if he was unable to focus, reflect on or project any emotion for an effective length of time. On the few occasions that I saw him express something akin to anger, it was like a sudden violent explosion of rage which lasted only a few seconds, as if he had no tolerance for it and had quickly to throe it out before having had time properly to feel it internally. Such explosions did not seem to be directed against real people in order to have any violent impact on them; instead his rage was simply ejected and scattered around at no particular object when he thought that he was not being observed.

By now he seemed used to my presence at least and I think that on the whole he probably recognised me. He certainly recognised my bead necklace. I was aware of this and so I always remembered to wear it whenever I visited him. The moment I came in he smiled at it as if he had seen an old friend, then he usually grasped it and quickly brought it to his mouth and began one of his complicated licking rituals. When I came back after the holiday my necklace was no longer an 'old friend' and he just stared at it rather blankly and briefly while sucking his tongue as if he did not remember it at all. I don't think that he remembered me either. Mrs T also forgot that I was coming in spite of my having phoned just the day before to arrange a visit. So I was left with the maid who told me how Martin had been teething during the summer, how he was now walking continually and only seemed happy when wearing his shoes.

It was also after this same holiday, when Martin was about ten months old that, to my great joy and relief I began to observe some changes in his father. As I have described, he became kinder to me and, much more important, he now seemed to treat Martin with more affection, interest and respect. The first time that I saw Martin holding someone's hand it was his father's; the first time that I really saw him look at someone it was also at his father; the first time that I saw him show any reaction of being hurt by someone leaving, again it was when his father had to go back to work after having been present during the earlier part of the observation. (Martin was then about eleven months old.) As he left, Martin struck the door several times with a miserable expression on his face. "Daddy" was the first word he uttered in my presence when he was about fifteen months old. He said this just after his father had left one day; he stood in front of the door and said "Daddy" several times in a soft voice, as if talking to himself and at the same time he pulled his hair violently and scratched his face as if terribly wounded and hard hit by an inexplicable loss or by a pain whose source he could not quite locate.

These were gleams of hope compared with the gloom of all the rest. After the summer, apart from his desperate, endless, restless walking, he looked even more blank and also terribly fat. He smelled unpleasant, was covered with scratches, and he constantly and noisily sucked his tongue. He nevertheless learnt a small repertoire of tricks which he would perform when asked by his mother. This seemed to reassure her greatly. He would clap his hands, twirl around, dance in a circle when she sang "ring-a-ring-a-roses". Sometimes he would make a mistake and his performance was the wrong one, not the one asked of him. Everyone laughed, but Martin just looked confused and bewildered and was suddenly paralysed with terror and utterly unable to move in the middle of his pathetic efforts.

Often he would smile at people with a mechanical gesture. Sometimes he would placate people by giving them some of his possessions, as when, the moment he saw me, he would hand over the 'precious' piece of banana that he was holding – all this done, I believe, to keep me quiet and at bay rather than to initiate a possible game or exchange.

Food still remained his obsession and he was forever in quest of it. He was on solid food by then and was beginning to eat by himself. I noticed how he would literally throw food, water, beverages into his mouth, gobbling and gulping them down in a trice. This was particularly evident with water and liquids in general; with solids he alternated between this kind of behaviour and his usual wrapping and rubbing with his tongue. Then, if given the chance, he would throw away the plastic cup or container from which he had just been drinking, projecting it through the air with the speed of a missile. One had the definite impression that eating and taking something in could not be a gradual and natural process for him (anatomically and physiologically, so to speak). It had to happen in a split second, without his perceiving the process; he suddenly felt satiated without any recognition of the 'object' which he had just taken in. The container was so quickly thrown away out of sight that it might as well never have been presented within his orbit. Present reality was neither seen nor respected. One somehow had the feeling that he travelled back in time to a state of illusory self-sufficiency and autonomy, to a state of omnipotence like the illusory autonomy of a foetus whose needs are 'magically' fulfilled even before they are felt, with no object in sight.

On the other hand his muscular ability became more and more marked and this somehow projected him into the future as, from this point of view, he was remarkably forward, if not unnaturally advanced, for his age. His present condition alone, perhaps understandably, seemed intolerable to him. In fact his muscular activity was exceptional also in the sense of being in some way bizarre. For instance, he would never use the support of his hands to stand up, nor would he stretch out and push his hands forward whenever he fell – he literally fell flat on his face. He hardly ever bent his knees, not even when he had to stoop to pick something up. This gave to his gait a mechanical, robot- or armour-like quality, as if he were built out of metal with rigid, rusty joints which could not bend in any way harmoniously. He did not seem to possess or to have assimilated into himself and into his body any idea of support and protection. He appeared to have no idea of two separate parts, of two separate entities working together. [When he was about eleven months old the doctor suggested having him X-rayed as he seemed unable to bend some of his fingers, especially the thumbs.] The various parts of his mind and body were quite uncoordinated in their development; some were too forward, some were too backward, some were almost atrophic, others were hypertrophic, all in a disjointed, artificially-assembled unity.

Martin's hyper-developed muscular activity and his extraordinary speed in moving and walking also served him more and more as an aid in getting away from people and unwanted situations: now he could simply leave and whenever he did this he did it very quickly. As his grandmother once said, "Martin, he doesn't walk, nor even run . . . he quite simply flies . . ." But 'flight' was not always available to him and often, when confronted with someone or something that caused him suffering, he would just remain there, paralysed and rooted to the ground.

When he was eleven months old his mother became pregnant and this was something that he could not easily get away from. The main effect of her pregnancy seemed to be to elicit from him some interest in the inside of things. Up until now I had almost only seen him explore the surface of objects. One of his favourite games was to try to juxtapose or make two surfaces adhere to one another. He would also bang the two surfaces violently against one another, as if objects were composed only of surfaces and that they either fitted perfectly and adhered as if they were just one surface, or they collided and banged and crushed one another. (I actually saw him do this twice with two ashtrays until he managed to crack them beyond repair.)

But now, on his mother's pregnancy, he seemed to have become aware of the fact that objects could also have an inside and not only a surface. Nevertheless his interest in the inside of objects seemed a superficial one; now he would often touch the inside of a bin or explore the inside of his cup, or (as I described before) he would crush his fingers trying to reach inside a drawer. As his mother's pregnancy became more visible I think it also became 'crushingly' evident to him how the inside of her body was now occupied by another object, by someone or something else, while he himself was clearly outside. He then desperately began to try to go against the evidence and reality in the hopeless attempt to travel back into, and regain his position and his illusory unity with, her body. He would bang his head against her pubis or her stomach while holding on to her thighs, striving to push his way inside. On a few occasions I also saw him try to push his head between the maid's legs as if, almost promiscuously, 'any' body would do. Alternately, he would hide inside an old cupboard and literally spend hours inside in complete darkness, stiff and immobile like a corpse inside a sealed coffin. Nothing outside seemed of any interest to him, and whenever anyone tried to drag him out he would look petrified with terror.

Nor was pregnancy an easy matter for his mother. She either felt terribly sick or was continually vomiting and often felt faint. On the few occasions that I saw her at that time she was mostly confined to her bedroom, sleeping or looking extremely pale and collapsed, almost unable to speak. She barely managed to tell me some of her fears, such as her terror of "losing all substance" or "liquefying and spilling all out". She told me how she felt terrified and confused by the stretch-marks and the other changes in her shape and her skin. She also told me, in her usual unemotional tone, that her body somehow felt strange to her and she did not know any longer who she was. Indeed it was truly difficult to tell who she felt that she was as I frequently had the feeling that she was totally identified with the product of her pregnancy, a product that must never move or change. Rather than being a baby or even a foetus, such a product at times seemed to be a kind of gelatinous embryo or an ovum, just beginning to move out of its undifferentiated background. Identified with it as she was, she seemed empty of any substantial or solid core, with a fragile, not even skin-deep surface outside. Any tiny breach or change in the surface could annihilate the beginning of life. It just made her collapse, making her non-existent content spill outside leaving her completely deflated and dissolved. The inevitable movement of life terrified her; she felt that it destroyed her and disturbed her death-like peace. All she seemed to want was to sleep and to be unconscious. She did then cancel the observations for about two months saying that she felt too ill to receive any visitors, and that all she needed was "darkness and peace".

One year to two and a half years

When I went back Martin was about fourteen months old and he was, if possible, even fatter, more sweaty and covered with scratches, with his tongue constantly protruding. When he saw me he flattened himself against the wall as if wanting to avoid a possible danger, such as being crushed, and behaving as if he was pretending to be a fly or a dot on the wall. Gloria was also present and I noticed how he copied all that she did, following her like a shadow wherever she went. This characteristic became more and more evident as months, and even years, went by. In particular he would copy and blindly follow any tyrannical leader, or any potential or actual persecutor. Later on, in the same way, he would blindly follow words and opinions and echo, parrot fashion, every single word said, flattening his individuality and showing a mixture of fear and total, undiscriminating admiration and adhesion to the 'aggressor'. By doing this I think that he was somehow trying to hide his true microscopic identity, his shadow of a self, so as to be left in peace to continue to live undisturbed behind the surface. He was trying both to give in to and give himself up to the tyrant so as to placate and avoid further, probably worse, persecution. But also, in a sense, he was achieving a kind of illusory unity with the tyrant in a way which reminded me very much of his solitary orgies where he was both tyrant and victim fused in the same person, inflicting pain on himself. But in this type of total, illusory fusion with the tyrant, the dimensions of his former self were reduced to almost nothing, to less than a minute dot. Now he was all-powerful but also, in a sense, he himself was no more.

It next became even more striking how he would never recognise his own reflection in a mirror but would just look at it in open-mouthed bewilderment as if he did not know who he was. Some years later, when he was almost seven (see Observation One) I once saw him with Mark, his younger, much more determined brother whom he also at times seemed to be following like a shadow. I was much struck by the fact that he now seemed to be the mirror image of his brother: the same size, same height, same weight (he was now rather slim), the same features, the same clothes, etc. You could only tell the difference from their behaviour, Mark being the undisputed leader, and from a few marks of inferiority in Martin as he was now wearing glasses and suffering from alopecia.

It also became more and more noticeable how Martin was ever on the alert, quickly trying to decipher and to anticipate what other people might want or expect from him, so as not to be caught unprepared. I observed, on quite a few occasions, how he was listening to what other people were saying to each other and then, picking up just a phrase or a name or a bit of the conversation, he would do something quite out of context that no one would ever have had the intention of asking him to do. For instance, one day his mother was talking to me about some chair. As he heard her say the word "chair" he ran and sat on a chair. Then as she continued on the topic he sat on another one, then another and so on, always watching her expression and trying to make out whether this was what she might have in mind for him. Then he remained sitting on a chair long after she had gone away. Sometimes he would laugh, pathetically out of context, or too soon or too late, with obviously forced laughter. He would blindly execute any order and go on endlessly and dutifully performing this task, unable to stop until he had received a counter order. One day, for instance, his mother asked him to pick up and put away a few toys that Gloria had dropped on the floor. He did this immediately; he frantically picked up all the other toys in the room; then all the other things that were lying about on the floor in the rest of the flat, and threw everything into the same box. When his mother noticed this she burst into laughter and said, "But just look at what he is doing . . . stop it, Martin . . . go and wash your hands now . . ." which he did, and then went on endlessly doing so, like some kind of crazed computer or broken robot.

Not surprisingly I hardly ever saw him at play and on the few occasions that I did see him engaged in something akin to play it had more the character of an endless, dutiful, trying occupation. Even something which might have begun as a game, with some spontaneity, was in the end transformed into a repetitive, mechanical, 'dead' activity. For example, one day some months later he pretended to shoot me and I pretended to fall. He smiled, openly amused, but then he went on pretending to shoot me for the rest of the observation and what had originally started as a spontaneous game was soon changed into a monotonous, stereotyped, emotionless activity.

His emotions or spontaneous gestures too seemed to exhibit the same degree of non-spontaneity and repetition. His responses always followed or went back to the same old patterns, a little like the pre-programmed responses of a simple computer that would reject anything outside its programme. On a few occasions he started with some spontaneous, potentially friendly and outgoing gesture; he would stretch out his hand as if wanting to touch my face or hair, but then he would stop half-way through, paralysed in mid-air, and soon afterwards his hand would slowly be withdrawn. Sometimes his after-reaction would be to go back to his familiar, routine, self-tormenting activities. On a number of occasions I saw him withdraw even further than that. This happened when I was sitting near him on the end of the bed; after attempting to touch me he looked terrified and pushed his head violently inside his pillow, at the same time moaning and trying to wrap it around himself like a safe cocoon. The same thing happened when one offered him something he clearly liked, such as an orange or a biscuit; he would refuse the offer and go into 'retreat', but would probably pick it up later on when he was alone. He certainly seemed to prefer and find safer the loneliness and refuge of a solitary, narrow, enclosed, well-known, unchangeable and predictable world to the hazards of opening up to the world of people and the risks of moving and living in it.

When he was about fifteen months old he formed a particularly strong attachment to his coat. He would always wear it at home and whenever anyone tried to remove it he screamed as if being skinned. To avoid this he usually tried to run off and be alone. It was only when he thought he was alone that I saw him, on just two occasions, express some feeling, though in an indirect, secretive way. One day when he was about nineteen months old I saw Gloria nag and torment him with all sorts of prohibitions, remarks and orders; Martin just followed, almost paralysed. As soon as she left the room he rapidly, almost frantically, touched all the forbidden articles and sketchily, symbolically performed all the prohibited actions; then, pretending to be 'innocent', returned to his paralysed state and waited for her to return. Another time he was nagged both by Gloria and by his mother and, as usual, he did not react in any way. Then, when they started talking to one another and forgot him for a while, he quickly availed himself of the opportunity, ran out of the room, violently kicked his ball (which he had spotted out of the corner of his eye), then quickly returned and stood there waiting for whatever might happen next, making sure of not having been seen.

But as time went on I became certain that he knew that I knew and observed him with benevolent eyes; he also knew that nothing 'bad' could be expected of me. Most of the time I had the impression that for him I was just part of the furniture, like a solid desk or table, something that would not act or react hostilely but would just be there available to him. At times, though, I had the impression that for him I represented something more than a mere article of furniture – a more solid, more human object which he could sporadically and tentatively lean on. Indeed, he sometimes actually leant against my legs and he would 'cling' to my eyes. A little later he learnt my name and on a few occasions, when all around him was in total confusion, I heard him utter and repeat it to himself as if trying desperately to evoke and hang on to some safe, steady memory. My bag, as earlier my necklace, also became an object of attraction to him; he usually smiled at the sight of it although not daring to touch it until I had made the first move and offered it to him, bringing it within his reach and encouraging him to take it. He would then tentatively explore it with a shy smile, ready to retreat fearfully into apparent static indifference should it contain something unexpected or frightening, or should his tentative explorations cause an equally frightening, unexpected reaction.

During those rare moments I had the impression that I was observing a tiny baby emerge from a hard, artificial shell and recognise with a smile of relief that a suitable object was now present to protect, hold and contain him in an appropriate new way. If encouraged and offered another kind of containment, a human and mental one, he could now dare to run the risk of starting to relate to an object outside his narrow orbit of tight control. He could now risk coming out and could leave behind his suffocating, inadequate and growth-impeding shell.

How Martin, underneath this armour, was still frantically and desperately searching for an object that could give him such containment was, I think, well represented in other behaviour which I had sometimes observed. He was expert at spotting and picking up any tiny neglected items (such as a crumb of biscuit, a bit of paper or a button) which had been dropped and abandoned on the floor (particularly in the kitchen). He would then immediately take it and run frantically from container to container, trying desperately to find a suitable one. He would run from his cup to a glass, to a tin, to the dustbin, putting his 'precious' bit momentarily in each of them and then he would move quickly on to the next receptacle. But none would do, till in the end he dropped and forgot about it and then usually ran out of the room. A parable, alas, of the story of his life!

When he was sixteen months old it also became clear how he had been picking up and collecting bits and pieces of all sorts of conversations (probably having done so all along). He suddenly began to talk and came out quite unexpectedly with the most extraordinary 'salad' of words. He poured out a confused and disjointed mass of undigested, disconnected, unassimilated fragments and then, to my amazement, quickly relapsed into silence, as if his long 'talk' had only had the function of getting rid of some indigestible, incomprehensible, useless stuff. And as time went on I witnessed several of these sudden and confused evacuations (a reversal of the process of continually swallowing huge amounts of indigestible, meaningless food).

Soon he began 'swallowing' and collecting words and names as if they were concrete possessions. Towards the end of his second year I would often observe him listening eagerly and almost secretively, like an eavesdropper, to any conversation, trying to grasp or grab as many isolated words as he could. In a whisper he would then proudly recite to himself the long, meaningless list of his newly acquired 'possessions'. He seemed to regard his new skill of talking as yet another tool in his desperate effort to master, control and keep at bay the surrounding world. Armed with speech (as previously he had been armed with his increasing muscular strength and control) he could now defend himself better and fight better for what he wanted. The purpose of communication seemed to play little part in his efforts to master and control the world of language; I rarely saw him talk to people around him while, on the other hand, I often saw him talk to himself or literally talk to the blank walls.

Word-collecting seemed to have the same restless, compulsive quality as his walking or eating which he appeared to do without any pause, pleasure or time for reflection. It also became evident (particularly in the following months and years) how he would use words as labels to catalogue and put in separate, well-defined compartments objects, feelings and events. Once he had found the appropriate word-box he felt safe and relieved that the 'thing' was under control. (This reminded me of his earlier controlling, and in a way 'defining' everything with his tongue.) Needless to say, in this kind of control the label, the surface, the sound, the reference of words was much more important than their possible deeper meaning, their possible connection with feelings and emotions. Often (at least while I observed him regularly), he would pathetically fail in his efforts at defining words and frequently attributed the wrong name or the wrong meaning, eliciting the usual outburst of laughter or comment on his stupidity from the people around him, while he just looked terrified and bewildered; it often seemed that he was unable to symbolise properly and he used many symbolic equations.

Moreover speech became, like his earlier smiles, a kind of mechanical duty. He again learnt his lesson in a computer-like way and fed back the appropriate, predictable answer devoid of phantasy or imagination. Repetition and imitation became increasingly evident. There was little sign of thought or feeling in his flat uninteresting way of talking. Speech, I think, was used by him as a kind of diaphragm, a barrier or wall of pseudo-normality and pseudo-relation to keep other people at a distance so that he could continue living undisturbed in his solitary, empty, silent world. He would wrap himself round with words in just the same way as earlier he had used his tongue to create a kind of covering membrane or almost muscular protection for himself. All these characteristics, in so far as I could tell from my infrequent contacts with him, continued to persist in the ensuing years. But before giving an obviously sketchy description of my impression of his subsequent development I would like to go back briefly to the last few months of my regular weekly contact with him.

Apart from the new developments in his speech the general picture remained pretty much unchanged up to the time that I left: he was still fat, blank, insensitive to pain, sweating profusely. But at least one major change took place in his life outside: the birth of this brother Mark when he was about nineteen months old. It was just before the summer that Mrs T told me that she was going to arrange for Gloria and Martin to stay with her parents in a house in the country for at least a couple of months. My visits were thus interrupted just before Mark's birth. As I was leaving, Mrs T promised to phone me and said laughing, "I will phone you to tell you its sex!"

In the event Martin stayed away until about the end of October and when I resumed my visits he was about twenty three months old. In the meantime, since my last observation, Mrs T's collection of *putti* had increased to an incredible extent. Martin did not seem to recognise me although he soon appeared to take a liking to me. He was constantly following, repeating and copying everything Gloria did or said. He also busily labelled everything in the way I have described. I didn't see Mark for quite a while; apparently he was always sleeping. I almost doubted his existence for a while as he was so rarely mentioned and life in the family seemed to go on more or less unchanged. Martin too, at least on the surface, didn't seem to be affected by the event. I only saw Mark briefly on three occasions when I was struck by his resemblance to Martin and by the fact that he also sucked his tongue. Martin behaved in a very kind and polite way towards him; he would gently stroke Mark's face calling him, "sweet little thing", he would ask about his health and his sleep; he would comment on his rashes and his movements, but there was no genuine spontaneity in these overtures. He seemed to have pathetically over-learnt his lesson. Under the surface of a too-perfect adaptation he appeared to want to obliterate and neutralise the event and to remain untouched. Just before I left, another important event took place apparently leaving him quite unaffected; the maid became pregnant and, deserted by her lover, attempted suicide in a toilet at Tottenham Court Road Underground. Her life was saved but she left the family. Mrs T replaced her by her sister who looked like an ugly copy but who dressed and behaved like a strict nun. On the surface Martin seemed not to have even noticed the change, using his usual strategy to obliterate it.

On my last observation almost all his resources and defensive measures were, as it were, displayed as in some sad parade and their failure too was pathetically evident. On this occasion he was sweating profusely, smelling unpleasant, and sucking his tongue constantly. He did not recognise his reflection in the mirror. His eyes were blank and he kept moving restlessly and frantically. He jumped off a chair without bending his knees or bringing his arms forward and he fell flat on his face showing no reaction to the pain. A little later when his mother entered he laughed loudly but this had no connection with anything that she said or did. When she ate some grapes he screamed in terror as if he had been bereft of life. He next gulped down a huge amount of food and when alone violently scratched his face. When Gloria came in he followed her like a shadow. She asked me to read her a story and he frantically repeated everything I said, pathetically distorting almost every word and certainly he was not following the meaning of the story. A little later his father came in and Gloria asked him to throw her up in the air. Martin was obviously terrified yet asked him to do the same. In the air he looked paralysed with fear and when once more on firm ground he continued gyrating for a while, vividly illustrating his muscular way of trying to protect himself and to neutralise the shock. Then, in response to his mother's request, he began to pick up all the articles strewn on the floor and he went on doing that relentlessly until I left and did not react in any way to my leaving. I departed feeling very sad, an impotent witness of a long, hopeless saga, in which Martin's life had the quality of a nightmare rather than of a dream.

The following years

This nightmare unfortunately continued during the subsequent years although I now saw Martin only about once a year. Therefore my impressions of his subsequent development can only be rather sketchy and probably superficial, particularly if compared with my previous close observation of him. Given the kind of absent-minded and forgetful attitude of his mother, I could not often elicit much information about his behaviour or significant events between my visits so that each time my subsequent observations remained isolated. Martin's continued state of retreat became manifest as time went by. He seemed at least as impervious to people as before, apparently untouched by emotion and insensitive to any kind of pain. His old obsessive controlling rituals to keep people, things and feelings at bay continued unabated, although perhaps in slightly different forms (for instance, his use of the rosary in the observation which follows). Physical movement still helped him to get away from people while at the same time building up a muscular protection and isolation for his inner self.

During many of my later observations he was almost always on the move. As years went by his withdrawal more and more took on the quality of superior detachment. When not blank his expression would now be indifferent and aloof, or sly and oblique with an imperceptible smile on his lips. It was much the same kind of smile that I had seen before on the maid's face, or his father's when early on Mr T seemed to believe that his secret and perverse world was so superior to that of poor people who did not know, such as Martin or myself.

During the observations Martin tended to withdraw into secretive activities while at the same time keeping a distant eye on the rest of us. Increasingly he had the look of a faraway spectator from another world rather than of an active participant in life who would now and then glance secretly at everything around him but continue to live, apparently unperturbed, in his own isolation. He still tried to hide behind people, following them like their shadow. He seemed afraid of being caught unprepared or off guard. He never asked for anything and soon began to help himself, stealing other people's words or trying always to anticipate their moves and their plans. In all this he looked increasingly like someone desperately trying to be cunning rather than someone eager to learn. I often thought, in the following years, that had I just seen Martin for the first time, without knowing of his nightmarish early history, I would probably have simply judged him to be an arrogant, rather disagreeable little fellow. For a few years he was able to keep up an appearance of normality and to hide behind the façade of superficially conventional behaviour. He was on the whole a dutiful, rather scholastic and pedantic student. But soon the surface began to crack and the underlying deficiencies began to show. His teachers began to notice that he "couldn't keep things in" (to quote Mrs T) nor could he make "meaningful links". His capacity for imagination was found to be rather poor. It was evident from what his mother told me in her own unperturbed, absent-minded way that at times Martin would show a somewhat faulty capacity to symbolise and tended to make concrete, bizarre links. However, since he was young no one seemed to worry much about his inability to learn. On the other hand people began to notice other cracks, such as his apparent indifference and strangeness. Soon it also became apparent that cruelty was now part of his hidden world; he began directing his viciousness against 'poor' and inferior people, for instance the numerous servants of the household. With such people he reversed his usual shadowy, passive role and acted like a sadistic and spiteful tyrant (see Observation One). Later (see Observation Two) he reserved the same kind of treatment for his youngest brother, Leo. But I should like now to pass on from this account of Martin's later development and turn instead to report two observations in detail. These are probably self-explanatory and need no comment; in any case, because of the sparsity of my contact with the child it is preferable, I think, that the reader should form direct impressions of his own.

In the first observation Martin was seven years old and Mrs T was about to give birth to the other baby, Leo, in just a few days' time.

Observation One

I had telephoned Mrs T the previous day and she had answered. When I told her who I was she said, "Oh, it's you . . ." I asked her how she and the rest of the family were and she said, "I have lots of news . . . plenty of new things have happened . . . I am pregnant for the fourth time (she says this laughing) . . . the baby will be born in a fortnight . . . you know it will be another Caesarean . . . Dr S as usual . . . but then this will be the last time . . . Martin is quite well . . . he is doing well at school . . . his teacher is pleased with him . . . then you know my husband had an internal haemorrhage . . . he is all right now . . . but I can't tell you . . . just think that he had just come back from Paris . . . then during the night he had an acute stomach ache and he vomited . . . and it was getting worse . . . so I didn't know whom to call . . . so I called a doctor from the Casualty Department . . . and he came and said that it was just nothing . . . can you imagine . . . but then he was really ill and he stayed in bed . . . then the following day I rang a friend of mine . . . he is a doctor and works at Guy's . . . and I told his symptoms . . . and he was very worried . . . he said 'I don't like it at all' . . . and he told me to keep him in bed and not to move him and that he was coming to see him. Then he decided to admit him into hospital . . . and they examined him . . . by now he was vomiting blood . . . so he was immediately taken into the operating theatre and Dr V operated on him . . . he is fantastic . . . he is like a god . . . the operation lasted seven hours . . . I can't tell you the fright . . . but then it all went well . . . and he has recovered completely . . . can you imagine, he could have died . . . but now he has to go in for check-ups from time to time for at least six months . . . he will have another operation about the end of the month . . . you know when I will be back from hospital and everything . . . but you know he is quite well now . . . but just think what might have happened . . . it happened in December . . . and I was already pregnant . . . so you can imagine . . ." I said that I was really terribly sorry about all this. We then arranged to meet the following day.

I ring the bell and a woman in her late fifties comes to open the door. I have never seen her before. She looks at me in a rather unfriendly, almost suspicious way, but does not say anything. I ask her if Mrs T is at home and she says, "Yes", nodding her head. Then we hear Mrs T calling me from the sitting-room. She is on the phone. She asks me to take a chair, but then she goes on talking. I think she is speaking to a friend. She keeps saying things like," Yes . . . of course . . . but can you imagine . . . oh yes . . ." and she goes on like this for about five minutes. I notice that she has put on a bit of weight, quite apart from the pregnancy. Her hair is shorter. She is wearing a pair of blue trousers, very tight at the ankle and a maternity blouse. While phoning and during most of the observation she keeps her left hand over her stomach. She looks very pregnant.

I look around and I am struck by the incredible number of new sculptures representing babies or small cherubs, all life size. They are everywhere; some are hanging from the ceiling, others are wrapped up like mummies, some have wings, some look more like dolls. The overall impression is quite macabre. I estimate that there are more than sixty. Otherwise the room looks much the same. Then Mrs T finishes her phone call. As she puts the receiver down she smiles at me and shakes my hand saying, "Hallo, Sandra, how are you . . ." I say that I am well and then give her the box of chocolates which I have brought with me. She smiles and says, "Thank you . . . you are always so kind . . ." and she holds the box for a moment without opening it and without looking at me. She seems lost in thought; then she says, "The children are downstairs in the garden . . ." Then she stands up and walks to the kitchen and I follow her. While walking she says, "Gloria is away . . . she is with my mother . . ." then she enters the kitchen and goes to the window. The woman who opened the door is there and she looks at us, then goes out. Mrs T points at the children down in the garden and says, "There they are . . ." I see Martin and Mark. They are both riding bicycles and they look very much alike; actually I cannot even distinguish which one is Martin from that distance. Mrs T calls them and they both look up. She says, "Martin, Mark, come upstairs . . ." Mark says "No", then Martin also says "No". Mrs T says, "Come on, Martin . . . look who is here . . . this lady has come on purpose to see you . . ." Mark says, "But then we'll come back and play again". Then they look at each other a moment and they both run upstairs. They run very fast and appear almost immediately.

In the meantime Mrs T has gone back into the sitting-room and I have followed her. We both sit down. The children come in running. Martin has grown quite a lot. He has lost a bit of weight and almost looks thin. He is wearing glasses and I notice some bald patches in his hair. He now looks very much like his father. His expression is somehow half-cunning, with a half smile on his lips as if he knew what was going on; he never seems to look anyone directly in the eyes. He conveys an impression of self-assurance and of subtle, superior detachment. Mark resembles him. They are dressed the same except for the colour of their sweaters. Mark talks more and is more direct — indeed he is the first to enter the sitting-room and is the first to look at me. His mother tells him to say hello and he does so; then Martin comes in and stands near the table. He says hello, but without looking at me and then almost immediately, and without looking at his mother, he says, "I want some chocolate." His mother takes my box of chocolates (it was on her chair and she had put it by her side) and she shows it to them saying, "Look . . . Sandra has just brought you some . . ." He looks at the box and I have the impression that he says "No", but I am not sure because he hardly moves his lips. Mark goes near the box and touches it. Martin looks at him. Mrs T looks at them and says, referring to Martin, "He is well . . . Have it, Martin . . ." He doesn't even look at the box or touch it and says, half-smiling, but always without looking and with his lips closed, "I can't open it . . ." Mrs T says, "Come on Martin, you can open it . . .", and she begins to unwrap the box. Mark takes over. Martin stands near looking at him and at the box and says, "It is all paper . . ." Mrs T laughs and says, "No, it is not all paper . . ." Mark seems quite excited and says, "Yes, it is all paper . . . here is some paper . . . and here's some more paper . . . it is all paper", and he giggles and Martin repeats, "It is all paper . . ." Then Mark says, "Oh, here are the chocolates", and he takes one. Martin takes part of the plastic wrapping and says, but almost in a whisper, "I don't like this one, it has already been burst . . ." (I think that he is referring to the fact that the plastic wrapping is made of plastic bubbles), and he drops it. Mark takes another chocolate and then Martin also takes one. Then he folds the wrapping and makes it into a thin kind of stick, and approaching his mother, but still without looking at her, he starts rubbing her arm lightly with the paper, but almost in a secretive way. She says, "Tell Sandra what you do." He doesn't say anything. She says, "Tell her the name of your school", and he tells me the name of his posh school without looking at me. She says, "Tell her what class you are in . . ." and he says, "First Primary . . ." She says, "He is good . . . actually very good . . . very, very good . . . well, no, I don't want to exaggerate . . ." and I notice that while he is talking to me and I am looking at her, Martin looks at me. Mark says, "Let's have some more chocolate", and Martin goes near him smiling and says, "Yes, let's have some more chocolate." Mrs T says, "Come on, . . . you should first offer some to us". Martin gives a chocolate to Mark (still half smiling) and says, "Have one." Mrs T says, "No, give one to us . . . come on . . ." and Martin then gives the box to her. She offers me a chocolate and, while doing so, she says, "He is madly independent . . . you know it is crazy how independent he is . . . he can even prepare his own food . . . the other day he made himself a pie . . . he does everything for himself . . . even his food . . . and he knows everything . . . he helps me . . . he knows how the washing machine works . . . and the other day I didn't know how to open a tin of tomato juice and he did it. He really can do everything by himself . . ." looking quite lost in thought while she was saying this.

Martin meanwhile is standing near the table with his arms at his sides apparently watching Mark who is playing with the chocolate box lid, but in fact I think he is listening to our conversation. Then Mrs T looks at him and says, "Show Sandra your cat . . . he has got a cat . . . he chose it himself . . ." Mark goes out of the room first and then Martin follows suit and comes back almost immediately holding a large grey cat in his arms. He puts it down at his mother's side and starts stroking it, standing some distance away from it. Mrs T says, "Now I must tell you an extraordinary story . . . we bought this cat from a shop . . . and he chose it . . . then after a few days I noticed that Gloria had some round spots on her arm . . ." Martin adds, but almost in a whisper, "so called, with an astronaut-disc shape . . ." She says, "Yes, that's right, and then I noticed a couple on myself . . . but I thought it was perhaps an allergy . . . then Gloria went away to the mountains with my mother . . . and they rang to say that she was covered with those spots . . . and I was covered too . . . so we went to the doctor . . . and just think we found out that we had caught ring-worm from the cat . . . I can't tell you . . . we also had to take medicine . . . thank God the rest of the family were all right and then . . . it was not finished" (while telling me this she laughs more and more sounding very amused) ". . . one morning I looked at the cat and coming out of his anus there was a kind of ball . . . you know, so big" (her gesture suggested something about as large as an orange) ". . . just think he had had a prolapse of the anus . . . you know with all his intestines sticking out . . ." While she is telling me all this Martin stands near her and continuously strokes the cat, but very slowly and, as I have described, almost keeping himself at a distance; he doesn't look at me. Then the phone rings and Mrs T answers it. She says, "Oh, hello, how are you? . . ." Then she tells me, "Sandra, you can go and play with the children in the other room . . . Martin go and show Sandra your toys . . ." Martin goes out of the room walking rather quickly and I follow him. Mark doesn't immediately follow us. I then notice that Martin has picked up another chocolate before leaving the sitting room, he eats it quickly and then puts the wrapping down on his bed.

Martin's bedroom looks more or less the same as before, only instead of a single bed there are now two beds. Martin points at a rather big toy that is on the floor and says, "That one is the Hulk." Then without looking at me he goes and picks up another toy, an action man. He pulls its arms and they get longer and longer and he smiles, then tells me, "Now try and hit it". I hit it and it is in fact terribly hard, almost painfully so. He just gives me a glance and half smiles. Mark comes in and approaches Martin. Martin starts hitting the chest of drawers and then the floor with his man and he hits quite hard. Mark looks at him and says, "You could break the floor with it . . ." Then Martin suddenly drops his toy in a corner and says to Mark, "Let's play karate . . ." and they immediately start pretending to fight. At first they stand, just pretending to hit one another; then Martin lies down on the floor, Mark sits on his stomach, and they pretend to be hitting one another. I notice that from time to time Martin gives me rapid, almost imperceptible glances as if to see my reaction. Then suddenly he pushes Mark away and says, "I have to go and do a wee . . ." He puts his arm round his brother and says, "You come too, my friend . . ." Mark says "no" and Martin seems taken aback by this but only for a fraction of a second and then he says, "Never mind then . . ." He approaches his bed and puts a small record on a toy record player that is there. I say that this is nice and is it his. He says "yes". The song is about some one who has to go to the bathroom and I do not remember more of the content, but the bathroom topic keeps being repeated. Martin plays it very loudly and then sits on a chair beside his bed where I am sitting. I again say something about the record. He doesn't reply. Mark in the meantime has left the room. I hear him probably going to the toilet and flushing it. Martin seems to curl up inside his chair. He starts rubbing his eyes with both hands. Then he puts his right index finger inside his mouth and seems to be touching his gums with it, first on one side and then on the other, then he places it in the middle but without sucking it. Next he takes his glasses off and puts them down on the small table near him. For a moment he clenches his fists and covers his eyes with them. Then he once more puts his index finger in his mouth and rubs his eyes with the other hand. Mark returns and sits near him on the same chair, but Martin doesn't seem to react and Mark looks at him in a perplexed way. Mark continues to stare at Martin's index finger, frowns for a moment and then he too puts his index finger in his mouth but he still looks perplexed. He glances at Martin and then says, "Let's read the book with the riddles . . ." Martin picks up a book that was on the table and opens it, keeping it in front of his face so that I can hardly see him and he starts reading aloud. He reads out four riddles whose answers they already know so that as soon as he reads one they both answer together. Then he starts reading stories and continues to do so without stopping. Mrs T comes back and sits on another chair.

She is lost in thought for a moment, then she looks at Martin and says, "But you know I have to tell another strange story. One day I noticed that he had a kind of patch on his head . . . I thought it must have been some chewing gum . . . anyway it was still there later on . . . so I decided to send him to a dermatologist . . . but I sent him to another one . . . you know, not the first one that I told you about" (she is referring to the one who treated her for the ring-worm caught from the cat) ". . . as I couldn't find his phone number . . . I looked up the telephone directory and I saw that there was this one near here . . . so I sent him there with my mother . . . and they went there . . . and it was terribly crowded . . . so that they had to queue for something like two hours . . . in the end this doctor saw him . . . and just guess what he said . . . he said he is neurotic . . . and prescribed lots of tranquillisers for him . . . but can you imagine anything as crazy as that . . . it is crazy . . . you go there because of a patch in your hair . . . and he tells you that he is disturbed . . . and just think, giving him tranquillisers . . . I would never use them . . . I almost thought of going back and telling him that he was an idiot . . . but the idea of queuing up for two hours just to tell him that somehow put me off . . . then anyway in the end I found the phone number of the first dermatologist . . . and so I took him there . . . he said it was alopecia . . . just think how crazy . . . just a bit of common sense would have been enough to tell him that it was that . . . have a look at it." She goes up to Martin to show me some patches on his head; he frowns and continues to read. The telephone rings and Mrs T goes out to answer it. I hear her talking to someone who is asking for a reference for a housekeeper whom she employed a couple of months ago. She says that the woman was good and honest but not very clever at engaging the children's attention. She goes on talking for a while and Martin continues to read aloud, with his left arm round his brother's shoulders. Mrs T comes back and sits on the chair again. She says, "It was someone asking for references . . . you know, about a woman that was with us for about four months . . ." Then she looks lost in thought for a moment. I ask her if she has someone helping her now and she seems to wake up and says," Oh, yes . . . now I have a couple . . . they come from Ceylon . . . they are marvellous . . . you know they even prepare home-made cakes . . . just marvellous . . . they have just gone home for Easter . . . let's hope that they will come back . . . anyway I have this other person helping

. . . she has been around for ages . . . but this other woman they asked me about, you know she was honest and hard working . . . but with the children she was a disaster . . . not so much with the other two . . . but with him" (and she indicates Martin) "you know what I mind about is chiefly punctuality and education in the sense that they should behave properly . . . anyway this woman was telling him not to shout and then not to talk loudly . . . but then she was always talking in a loud voice herself . . . and he was saying, 'But why is she shouting?' . . . you know, things like that . . . she really didn't know how to deal with him . . . how to impress him . . ." At this point Mark stands up and says, "I want to go downstairs and play in the garden again . . . you promised . . ." She says, "Come on, wait a few more minutes." He says, "A few minutes have already passed . . ." The woman who had let me into the house enters and says in a rather annoyed voice, "What do you want me to do? Are we to go out now?" Mrs T says, "Just one minute . . . you know the lady doctor has come to see Martin . . . I don't now remember if you are a psychiatrist or a psychologist? . . ." I say I am a psychiatrist. The woman says, "Why? . . . because of his hair? . . . he needs treatment." Mrs T looks almost frightened and says, "Oh, no . . . not because of that . . . she has been seeing him since he was a baby . . . you know she wanted to see how a baby grows . . . actually a normal one . . ." The woman still doesn't look very convinced by this. Mark has now gone to open a drawer and takes a rosary out of it. Martin does the same, then Mark goes out and Martin remains for a moment holding his rosary. Mrs T says, "He has matured a lot since his father's illness . . ." I say how I remember that he was always fond of his father. She says, "Oh, no it is not that . . . he didn't show any distress or anything . . . but he was saying his rosary all the time . . . you know he picked up this habit from a Spanish maid . . ." She looks lost in thought again. The phone rings and she goes to answer it. Mark comes back and the woman asks, "Would you mind going out of the room . . . you know otherwise they will start showing off . . . you know they want attention . . . and I have to carry on getting them ready to go out . . ." and she rather abruptly closes the door behind me. I feel a little awkward and stand in the corridor. Mrs T continues to talk with someone on the phone about some antiques. She goes on for a few minutes, then finishes and asks me to follow her into the sitting-room. We go and sit there as before. She says, "It was someone asking me about some antiques . . . I am very interested in them . . . I like them very much . . . you know I also read a lot . . ."

We hear the doorbell ring and then we see in the distance a Singhalese couple coming in. Mrs T says hello to them from the sitting-room and asks them if everything went well and they say yes. She says, "Thank God they are back . . ." Then the other woman comes in followed by the two children and says, "We are going out now . . ." Mrs T asks Martin, "What are you taking with you? Your bike and what else?" He says, "If I take my bike I can't take anything else . . ." She says, "Oh, yes, you're right . . ." Martin is now near her and he slightly rubs his arm against hers. She says, "Be careful . . . don't climb the trees . . ." Then the woman says, "Let's go", and the boys follow her. Mrs T says, "Say goodbye to Sandra . . ." and they both give me a wave from the corridor but without looking back at me. Mrs T looks lost in thought for a moment and says, "It is difficult for Martin when Gloria is around . . . then he is left out . . . Martin is difficult . . . also with that other one . . . with the other woman he was doing things like threatening her with a knife . . . but what the dermatologist said is crazy . . ."

While speaking she is lost in thought. The phone rings and she answers it. From what I can gather it is a friend phoning her from Paris, asking her a lot of questions about another couple who have just arrived. Mrs T tells her that the situation was tense anyway as the man didn't want to marry the woman. They then talk of someone else and how he is now with a new girl friend and she is going to see him for a week-end. I feel a little awkward and start to look around the room. I examine several pictures of Mrs T and her husband, taken mainly at parties. Then I look at some of the wooden *putti*. Mrs T talks for about five minutes until she eventually tells her friend that they will meet anyway on Friday as the friend is coming to London and she will tell her more then. She finishes the call and looks lost in thought. I go back and sit down.

She remains silent for a moment, then she says, "But I have to tell you another adventure I went through last year . . . you know last year I became pregnant again. I don't mean this pregnancy . . . but another one . . . you know it was not planned . . . but never mind . . . I somehow knew I was going to have a fourth child . . . so I thought 'All right . . .' I went to see Dr S as usual and then just before the holidays started I began to bleed . . . we had already planned everything as we were going to the country . . . so I went to see Dr S again . . . and he said it was up to me . . . you know there was a risk . . . anyway I decided to go . . . also because I knew that near where I was going there was a hospital specialising in these things . . . so I went to see this specialist . . . but before going to see him I had some tests done . . . you know I felt that there was something strange . . . apart from the bleeding . . . you know the baby wasn't moving any more . . . anyway I had the results of this test . . . and the doctor there told me that the child inside was dead . . . I had an internal abortion . . . so then I went to see this other specialist and he just dismissed the results of the test and said it was not true . . . he told me to stay in bed, gave me a lot of injections and hormones to take . . . but I still felt that it was not right . . . you know, the baby wasn't moving at all . . . then when we came back I went to see Dr S's assistant as Dr S was on holiday . . . and they did another test with ultrasonic sound . . . and in fact the baby was dead . . . it was an internal abortion . . . and the same evening I started bleeding again and I went into hospital . . . and they did it . . . but I had to have an anaesthetic . . . you know how I hate anaesthetics . . . you know I hate things getting out of control . . . I only feel safe if I can have things under control . . . that is why I don't drink." I say that I am sorry about this and that things must have been very difficult especially with her husband also being ill. She says, referring to the abortion, "Oh, well, it wasn't too bad . . . it is just that I hate anaesthetics . . ." (While she had been talking about the abortion her voice didn't reveal much emotion; it was not very different from the tone of voice she always uses.) Then she says of her husband, "Yes, my husband . . . you know he always used to have quite severe stomach cramps . . . you know once he even vomited . . . and I told him that he should go and see a specialist . . . but he said that it was probably just a stomach upset . . . but then he should have seen a specialist for his stomach . . . anyway he never did anything about it . . . but it was lucky that he was here . . . can you imagine if it had happened while he was on the plane or while he was abroad on holiday . . . you know he likes to go to the islands on holiday . . . for instance he went to the Caribbean quite recently . . . thank God my friend went too." I say it must have been terrible. She says, "Yes . . . you know I was worried about him . . . and you know how one just thinks about other things as well . . . supposing something happened to him . . . I was also thinking about the economic situation . . . you know I was considering the economic situation . . . you know with four children . . . all my life . . . you know my style of life would have to change . . . so there was also that . . ." Then she pauses, looks lost in thought and says, "But you know I also went to see a neurologist . . . you know I always have this fear of going out . . . and last summer I felt really ill . . . I was at the seaside . . . I was terrified of going out . . . I was crying for no reason . . . and I was feeling sleepy all the time as well . . . you know I couldn't even go out of the house . . . or take a bus or anything . . . then we came back and one evening we were having people for dinner . . . while I was with all these people . . . I felt I couldn't move my arm . . . and then all this side of my face started feeling funny . . . and I also had the impression that I was finding it difficult to say the appropriate words . . . I can't tell you what a terrible fright . . . so the day after I went to see a neurologist . . . I also had a scan . . . but everything was normal . . . so the neurologist told me that it must all be psychological . . . so I went to see Dr R and we just had a few sessions . . . I actually saw him for two months . . . and then he said that it was all right . . ."

The phone rings again. She answers it and says that she will ring the caller back in five minutes as she is busy at the moment. Then she says, "But even now you know I find it difficult to go out . . . I can only stay in a familiar place . . . you know I still can't take a bus or anything . . . I find it difficult even going out shopping . . . but this year I decided that I would go to the mountains . . . I feel better there . . . and who cares about the sea . . ." She looks lost in thought. I say that I am very sorry about all this. She knows my opinion about Martin and should she decide to seek help for him or herself she knows she can count on me. I say that I must go. She asks me, "And how are you? . . ." I say that I am well. She asks, "And do you work with children? Is it possible to see when a child is ill? . . . I mean mentally ill? Is it true that it all depends on the parents?" I say that I don't think that this is completely true. She says, "Yes . . . I suppose so . . . I suppose you can only try to do your best . . ." Then again she looks lost in thought. After a couple of minutes she stands up and takes me to the door. I thank her very much and wish her all the best for the new baby and ask her to greet her husband for me. She says goodbye to me saying, "Goodbye Sandra . . ." and closes the door.

In this observation Mrs T's outpouring of every kind of horror and fear needs little or no comment. She tells me about her husband's haemorrhage, her baby's death, her fears of paralysis and collapse. Such shocking facts are confusedly mixed with other strange and factual horrors such as her cat's anal prolapse or the ring-worm incident, all told in the same social tone, giving them an even more unreal, nightmarish quality. While listening to all this it was really difficult for me to know whether I was being told of real events or phantasies. Though her social façade is apparently untouched and she speaks of these facts as if they were 'society news', one can get a glimpse of the kind of paralysing, visceral terrors and of the acute dangers of internal death lurking behind the surface, ready to pour out and overwhelm her. Her golden cocoon, while sheltering and anaesthetising her from all this, also feels like a death trap containing only illness, bleeding, still-birth and death.

It is becoming increasingly difficult to ignore Martin's impoverished development. Certainly the dermatologist and all the servants seem to realise this. His mother too, though she considers what the dermatologist said was crazy, seems at least to be aware of his being difficult and "madly independent". But he himself, moreover, seems frightened of what may be hiding behind his apparently detached, superior surface. In his derogatory "It is all paper", he seems to express his belief that this wrapping is perhaps just covering emptiness and falsity. When he says, "I don't like it . . . it's already burst", he seems to be afraid of the possibility of his shell bursting or deflating. Yet he still desperately tries to erect between himself and people an impenetrable, hard wall. As he says, challenging me to touch his invulnerable hulk, "Now try and hit it", knowing quite well that I will be the hurt one. His contact with his mother by now appears to be only a tenuous, cutaneous, almost imperceptible one, as when he rubs the piece of paper and later his arm against her arm. His pet likewise is cautiously kept at arm's length. Most of the time Martin seems to hide behind Mark whom he always follows like a shadow and copies. While in Mark's shadow he seems to be protected from exposure and fear. When Mark reacts unexpectedly, saying "no" to his request that they go together to the loo, he seems taken aback and bewildered. A moment later he seems to conceal his plea inside a repetitive song and his camouflage goes to the extent of not following Mark when he goes to the toilet. One has the impression that he would rather burst his bladder than be exposed again to rebuff. When alone with me he seems terrified, then retreats quickly inside his shell. He closes his eyes, curls up like a foetus and starts his habitual tongue rituals to neutralise my presence and prevent my getting in. Later, when Mark returns, he hides behind his book and a wall of continuous familiar words.

When Martin is about to go out his mother tells me about his reaction to the news of his father being in danger of death. Martin apparently did not show any anxiety or distress, but withdrew into one of his favourite rituals, reciting his rosary. This reminded me very much of earlier rituals with his tongue. But in this observation an organic illness, alopecia is now also present. While not aiming at any cause and effect explanation, I am struck by the fact that as well as this hair loss Martin seems to lose bits of himself in his cold retreat from the world. Clearly now his defences are 'patchy'. But in looking at his impassive expression coupled with the hair loss I am reminded of his early incapacity to elaborate and feel emotions at a mental level and of his earlier resort to physical evacuation through his skin. Not much else seems to have changed from that primitive state.

In this observation Mrs T says that Martin is doing well at school; probably it is difficult to detect clear signs of his learning difficulties at this stage. His obsessive cataloguing is shown when he describes his mother's round spots as "an astronaut disc shape". This kind of pedantic learning is often what is required of pupils of this age. Undoubtedly Martin would excel at repetition and memorisation; probably this ability dates back to his enclosing everything with his tongue. But given his difficulty in being open to experience, it is not hard to imagine that problems may already be there under the surface of scholastic learning.

Here is Martin a few years later, when he is just eleven and his "monstrous" difficulties are obvious to all.

Observation Two

I ring the bell and a rather short, fat man in his fifties comes to open the door. Although he is wearing ordinary clothes I put him down as a servant. I ask if Mrs T is at home and he replies deferentially, "Yes, the lady is at home . . ." I notice that he has a foreign, probably a Spanish accent. He goes to Mrs T's bedroom and I hear him say, "Someone is here for you . . ." As I enter the house I notice a slim, blonde young girl walk across the hall and then disappear into the sitting-room. (I cannot see her face and for a moment I think it may be Mrs T but then I realise that she is too slim and young-looking.) While I wait for Mrs T, I suddenly have the feeling that someone is observing me. I look over at the unlit area of the sitting-room and catch sight of a boy who is silently spying at me from the doorway. As our eyes meet he disappears, a sly smile on his lips. A minute later I hear a boy and girl giggling and talking together in the sitting-room. Mrs T comes back into the hall and greets me somewhat theatrically saying, "Hello, Sandra . . . how are you?" I greet her also and ask her how she is. She replies absent-mindedly, "Well . . . well . . ." and then goes into the corridor and I follow. She is wearing very heavy make up – layers and layers of heavy orange foundation, shocking-pink lipstick, thick gold eyeshadow and mascara. Her hair is cut rather short, pageboy style, and bleached to the point of looking almost white. She looks older and the overall impression is both grotesque and macabre. But what strikes me most is her dress. She is wearing an incredibly short black satin miniskirt. The top consists of a mediaeval looking black velvet bodice and a bright red Elizabethan type ruff, with huge Renaissance sleeves made of brightly coloured tartan satin; under the mini she is wearing a pair of black tights and a pair of high red boots; the impression is of an incredible mixture of styles, epochs and sexes. She approaches me and takes my coat. I say that I have a small box of chocolates for them. She thanks me saying, "Oh, thank you . . . you are always so kind . . ." then she calls out, "Martin . . . Gloria . . . come here . . . Sandra has brought some chocolates for you . . ." Martin runs along the corridor followed by Gloria. I see that he is in fact the boy that I had seen earlier and I realise that Gloria was the girl I had glimpsed in the hall. She is quite tall and very slim, with long blonde hair, and although her face is less attractive than when she was a young child she looks much more friendly and soft, and indeed she smiles at me a little shyly and thanks me while shaking my hand. Martin is also very slim, but not very tall. His hair is longish and curly and also cut pageboy fashion. He has a somewhat sly, oblique and superior expression and a half-smile constantly on his lips; at the same time he looks aloof and detached; in general throughout the observation he avoids looking directly at me.

On the few occasions that I catch him looking at me while I am talking or listening to someone else he immediately looks away, looks down or lowers his head. He moves rather gracefully and lightly, a little like an acrobat and as silently as an agile animal. During the observation he is constantly on the move. At times, however, he can also be quite clumsy and can suddenly look flabby and deflated. Like his sister Gloria he is wearing a jogging suit. He grasps my box of chocolates from his mother's hand and seems ready to run away but she says, "Say thank you and hello to Sandra . . . shake hands with her . . ." He shakes hands with me, without looking at me, still with a sly smile on his face, then he quickly runs away and disappears into the sitting-room followed by Gloria. I hear them laughing and joking together – it seems that each is trying to seize the chocolates. Mrs T looks absent-minded. She takes my umbrella.

At this moment Leo comes out of his room and runs into the corridor. Mrs T stops him and shakes him while smiling and saying, "Here he is . . . he is very good . . . he is an angel . . . he is my darling . . . do you know he goes to nursery school now . . . he has just started." Leo looks very much like his mother, with the same eyes and nose, the same fair complexion. His hair is cut like hers, is very straight and whitish. He giggles while his mother shakes him and then he runs back into another room. Mark now comes running along the corridor from yet another room and Mrs T says, though rather absent-mindedly, "He really is my darling . . . he is so good . . . he's also very good at school . . ." Mark looks at me a moment, then disappears again. I notice that he still resembles Martin; the same height and weight, the same hair, jogging suit and almost the same face, only Mark's face looks more open, with big, direct eyes and he often smiles and looks people in the face. Mrs T is still holding my coat and she now hangs it up and moves towards the area of the sitting-room that it still in darkness and she puts the light on. I follow her. Then she asks me, "Would you like a drink? . . . a Martini . . . some port . . . a coke . . . or some water?" I reply that I wouldn't mind a glass of water. She calls Martin (he is still on the other side of the room with Gloria) and she asks him to bring me some water. We sit down on the sofa. Martin is back in a second and he gives me a kind of tankard full of water, then runs away smiling. Mrs T calls him back laughing and says, "But what kind of glass did you bring for her? Look at it . . ." (she laughs again very loudly), "Martin, Gloria come here . . . come and play in this part of the room . . ." Martin and Gloria come quite near us and they continue to pretend to fight over the chocolates. Mrs T looks at them rather blankly, then she turns to me and says, "Gloria is good at school now . . . she has improved a lot . . . she had lots of problems at first . . . she has improved a lot, particularly in maths . . . her English is still a disaster . . . but she is very good at maths . . ." Gloria intervenes at this point and says, "Not very good . . . I am all right . . ." Mrs T smiles and then, pointing at Martin, says, "While he is a disaster . . . just a disaster . . ." Gloria now succeeds in grabbing the chocolates from Martin and she laughs loudly. Mrs T says, 'Stop it now . . ." Then again she turns to me and asks, "And what is your work now?" I reply that I am a psychoanalyst and that I work both with adults and with children. She asks, "Do you work privately?" and I say yes. She seems to be growing increasingly blank and remains silent a moment. Then she looks at Martin, who is now triumphantly holding the chocolates, and says, "Why don't you offer one to Sandra . . . and I also want one . . ." Martin pretends to throw a chocolate at me but she immediately says, "No, stop doing that . . . do it properly . . . come over here . . ." Then she turns to me saying, "I am very insistent about manners . . ." Martin now offers both me and his mother a chocolate and then sits down beside the sofa and starts doing something with Gloria, but I cannot see what it is as their backs are turned and also because Mrs T now starts talking to me. Referring to Martin she says, "But do you know that he knows how to cook?" Martin turns his head slightly towards us and says, "Don't . . . not my secrets . . ." and this time he no longer smiles. Mrs T merely shrugs and continues, "He prepared dinner for me the other night . . . and another time he made some bread . . . he is very good at it . . . he is also very clean and tidy . . . you know he cleans everything . . . everything is orderly . . . Gloria, no . . . she is a disaster . . . she has no interest in it . . . and she is not interested in anything, she is just a disaster . . ." Gloria now stands up a moment and says to me," It's true you know . . . cooking, it's not my thing." I drink some water and Mrs T looks at me; then she asks Martin to bring her a glass of water too. Martin runs out and again returns very quickly. Mrs T goes on to say, "But now Gloria is better at school . . . she likes French, Italian and maths. She is studying Italian as a second language . . . but he" (at this point Martin is back and is half hiding behind the sofa opposite us) "is terrible . . . you know he is just a disaster . . . his teacher is in despair . . . he doesn't write . . . his homework is terrible . . . he doesn't learn . . . and there are other things . . . such as that he can't distinguish . . . you know between situations . . . and things . . . for instance the other day . . . we were both in the car, with a friend of mine and she was driving . . . it was her car . . . and he said that it was an awful car . . . luckily she didn't mind . . . but you know you never know . . . I didn't find it at all funny . . . really he does not distinguish . . . for instance if I am here with a friend . . . you know sometimes friends come to see me . . . and they want to tell me personal things . . . such as affairs . . . or the story of their life . . . and he just stays there . . . you know it is not on my own account . . . I share everything with them . . . they know everything about my life . . . and I have no secrets from them . . . but not everyone is like that . . . the other children, they understand . . . they go away . . . but he doesn't . . . he likes swearing too . . . even in front of people we don't know . . . they might not find it funny . . . and you know how insistent I am about manners . . . you know, good manners, they're essential . . ." During all this time Martin was still half hiding behind the sofa with a rather stiff smile on his face, listening.

Mark now comes in and sits on the sofa opposite us; Gloria sits next to him; Martin sits on the floor on my left. He leans with his back against a large cushion and keeps the greater part of his body hidden under the small table that is in front of us (only the top of his shoulders and head show). Mrs T looks at him, then says to me, "But do you know that he has two rows of teeth? . . . I just found out the other day . . . feel how strange . . . tell me what you think of it . . . Martin show your teeth to Sandra . . . this lady is a doctor you know . . ." I feel rather embarrassed but feel his teeth and find that there are two supernumerary ones behind his front teeth and I tell her so. She says, "You see, his teeth are not regular . . . I've been thinking of bringing him to see a dentist . . . but why they are not regular . . . you see you are a monster . . . I've never heard of anything like that . . ." I say that it is not all that unusual. She says, "But he is strange . . . you are not normal . . ." For a moment Martin looks both frightened and angry and says "no", then he puts on his usual smile and says, "At least I shall always have some spare teeth . . . when I lose them again . . ." Mrs T says, "But no . . . you will not lose them again . . . you just lose them once . . . and what can I do now?" (She says this to me.) I reply that she could take him to see a dentist and perhaps have an X-ray done.

Again she repeats, "But about his teeth, it is monstrous . . . not normal . . . as with the school . . . they wanted to kick him out . . . he writes appallingly . . . he doesn't remember anything . . . you know, things that the teacher said just the minute before . . . he just cannot keep them in his head . . . he can't retain anything . . . and yet he is intelligent . . . he understands . . . though sometimes the meaning escapes him . . . his teacher is in despair . . . you know luckily it is a private school . . . you pay a lot of money . . . so usually they don't kick you out . . . he just can't pay attention . . . or keep his attention fixed . . . his teacher told me that the only way to obtain something from him is to threaten him . . ." During all this time Martin disappears more and more under the small table. He doesn't look at us and progressively the smile fades from his lips. Then almost in a whisper he says, "But why are you telling my secrets?" She seems rather annoyed at this and says, "No, these aren't secrets . . . I talk about the others as well . . . I spoke about Gloria just now."

She turns to me and goes on, "I have to be after him all the time . . . and he is so madly independent . . . he is also vicious with servants . . . but he has many friends . . . he is just like me . . . he is sociable like me . . . he likes parties . . . he gets lots of phone calls . . . he is very sought after . . . lots of girls phone him too . . . but for the rest, it's a disaster. Mark is different . . . he studies . . . he also has friends . . . but it is Martin who usually takes him with him to parties, you know . . ." Gloria has been listening carefully to all this, from time to time giggling with Mark or exchanging glances with him. Now she takes another chocolate and Martin immediately grabs the box and takes one too. Mrs T says, "No, give one to Mark." She also takes one and in a moment almost all the chocolates have gone.

Martin now approaches a huge baroque wardrobe and climbs up it with incredible agility. Mrs T looks at him and says, "Come down . . ." Martin says, "It's empty up here." She says, "Yes . . . of course . . . come down . . . you are a fucker . . ." Then she says to me, "You see now how he goes on." Martin now begins to perform lots of handstands and other capers, jumping acrobatically all over the place, almost non-stop. Mrs T says, "Stop it . . ." but then she looks more and more blank and absent-minded. Gloria and Mark get up and also begin to engage in acrobatics and in a trice the room seems to have become a huge circus. After remaining silent a few minutes Mrs T seems to wake up and says, "Stop it now . . ." a few times.

Eventually Mark and Gloria sit down on the sofa once more and Martin approaches his mother saying, "I will play that game now . . ." and he whispers something in her ear. She says, "Repeat that to Sandra as well." In my ear his whispers the word "tankard". Then he sits down at the small table as before, puts his hands over his eyes and face as if concentrating intensely. Gloria and Mark sit on the other side of the table and seem to be concentrating as well. After a few minutes Mark says, "I've got it now . . . it's the tankard . . ." Gloria says, "Yes . . . I also saw it . . ." Mrs T looks totally lost in thought now. Martin says, "Let's try again . . ." He whispers "candlestick" to me and to his mother and then he sits down again and concentrates. Again after a few minutes Gloria this time says, "I've got it . . ." she looks at Mark and after a couple of minutes he also says, "Hang on just a minute . . . yes, now I can see it . . ." Then they both say "candlestick". Mrs T suddenly seems to wake up and says, "But how did you do it? . . . I don't believe it . . . there must be some trick . . ." Martin shakes his head and Gloria and Mark react strongly saying, "No . . . there is no trick . . . he can do it . . . we found out ten days ago . . . when we were at the racecourse." Mark also says, "He is like Uncle B . . ." Mrs T smiles. I say that I remember her telling me that her brother-in-law devotes himself to para-psychology. She nods and says, "But come on, tell me your trick . . . I don't believe it . . . it is incredible . . . how did he do it?" (She says this to me.) Gloria says, "Come on, Martin, let's try once again . . ." Mrs T says, "Let's do it properly . . . you two go away . . ." but Gloria insists, "No, just once more like this . . ." Martin who has been silent all this while now whispers in our ears the word "shoe", and again seems to be concentrating. Mark says, "I can't get it this time . . . it gives me a headache . . . but hang on . . . probably I've got it . . . carpet . . . no something on it . . ." Gloria says, "I can't visualise it clearly . . ." Then Mark says, "boots". (I am wearing boots.) Mrs T says, "No, but nearly . . ." Gloria says, "Yes, now it's clear, it's shoe . . ." Mrs T says, "But this time you" (she is referring to Mark) "got it wrong." Both Mark and Gloria protest loudly saying, "Sometimes it can happen . . . sometimes one goes wrong . . . or perhaps the shoe is just part of the image . . ." Mark adds, "I saw the carpet . . . the shoe was only on the edge of it." Mrs T again says, "Incredible . . . I don't believe it . . . let's do it properly now . . ." This time Martin says, "Yes, if you like . . ." Mrs T says, "Gloria and Mark . . . go out . . . go into the kitchen, we'll call you . . ." We remain with Martin. He seems to be thinking what word to choose this time. Mrs T says, "Why don't you say 'ashtray' . . ." Martin says, "O.K. I'll say ashtray . . ." Mrs T calls Mark and Gloria back and again the whole scene is repeated, then after a few minutes Mark says "I've got it . . ." followed almost immediately by Gloria. Then they both point at the ashtray. Mrs T looks very surprised (at this point I do too). She laughs rather loudly and again says, "Incredible . . . how can he do it?" The telephone rings and she goes and answers (the phone is in a corner of the room). She says emphatically, "Oh, it's you . . . how are you? . . . it's been ages . . . tell me about everything . . ." Then, after listening to the caller for a couple of minutes she says, "Hang on a minute . . . I'll go into the other room . . . so that I can talk more freely . . ." As she goes out she says, "Forgive me, Sandra, but it is urgent . . ." She remains out for about half an hour. Gloria says to me, "Let's do it once more . . ." Martin gets up and after a minute's hesitation whispers in my ear, "chest of drawers", then he concentrates until Gloria says, "I've got it now . . . it's that", and points at a big chest of drawers that stands behind the sofa where she is sitting. Mark also says, "Yes, it's that . . . but now I've got a headache . . . it's the effort." Martin raises his head and gives me a half-glance. Gloria now says, "Yes, . . . it happened ten days ago . . . he can do it even through walls . . . I couldn't believe it . . . we were there and he guessed all the horses that were going to win . . . he is just like Uncle B . . . and he can transmit thoughts and images . . ." Martin, if anything, now looks a little embarrassed but then says, "Yes, sometimes I can predict things . . . like this morning I said that the car wasn't going to work . . . and it didn't . . ." Gloria says, "Yes . . . and then we were all late for school . . . they say that you can inherit the gift, particularly from your father's family . . . and their uncle is a medium . . . but I also know a woman who is like that . . . you know, the woman who comes to give the injections." te says this to her brothers.) "That ugly one . . . her lips are all strange . . . she is extremely ugly . . . she says she can talk to the dead . . . she even wrote a book . . . you remember that book?" (again said to her brothers) "The one on Socrates . . . she swears she can talk to him . . . and then she talks to her mother who is dead . . . she was very jealous of her two older brothers . . . but her mother keeps reassuring her . . . she says that she loves her . . . then she tells her that she can travel now . . . she can see many places . . . it's nice being dead . . . and her daughter too . . . she says that she can predict things." Mark says, "But it could all be lies . . . I can predict that mother will soon receive another phone call . . . you can't go wrong with that . . ." Martin now intervenes, "I can predict that shortly we shall be cutting capers . . . but I can't predict my lessons." Mark says, "My father is also able to guess things when he plays cards . . . he sees them . . . but Martin really can transmit images . . . like he did before . . . even if the experiment sometimes fails . . . like with the carpet instead of the shoe . . . that was because the shoe was on the carpet, but you thought the carpet was the important thing . . . but this gives me a headache . . . I'm going to have another chocolate." They all have another chocolate. Now there are only three left and Mark says, "Let's put them inside this box . . ." and he puts them in one of the many silver boxes that are on the table.

Gloria shows me a book that I hadn't noticed, hidden on the sofa behind her. She says, "I would love to predict all my lessons . . . perhaps not all of them . . . just those I don't like . . . Italian no . . . I like it very much." Martin now takes the lid off the empty chocolate box (it is quite big and made of tin). He stands up and looks at his reflection in it, then says, "This is like a mirror . . . the mirror is nicer than my image in it . . ." The other two appear not to listen to him. Gloria continues, "Mummy tells me that you live in Italy now. Where?" I reply that I live in Milan. She asks, "But is it true that it is very foggy?" I say it is. Then she asks me how to say, 'What's the time?' and 'What's your name?' She then says that she would like to show me her Italian book.

Mark asks me, "Do you remember us when we were small?" I say that of course I do and he immediately says, "Martin was very ugly as a baby, wasn't he?" I say that was not true. Martin again looks rather embarrassed, though only for a second; then he says, "Let's go and play cards . . ." Mark says no. Martin gets up and starts cutting capers, doing handstands almost non-stop and after a moment Mark joins in. Gloria says, "It is much better doing acrobatics in this room because of the carpet . . . in my room I just have a wooden floor."

Gloria then goes out to get her Italian book. She comes back, sits near me and asks me a few things like the Italian for clock, truck etc., and I tell her. After telling her three or four words she shuts the book and says, "But of course I don't know these . . . I haven't learnt them yet . . . I suppose I will learn Italian pretty easily . . . you know I just need to learn new words, I know the grammar quite well . . . I would love to go to Italy . . . I mean to go." In the meantime Mark and Martin continue with their acrobatics. Then Martin comes and sits on the edge of the sofa opposite me. He sits with his legs astride it as if he is riding a horse and Mark says, "Do you know that until very recently if he saw an illustration of a horse he would try to ride it . . . he just couldn't distinguish . . . or if one said 'horse' he would try to ride something . . . the illustration was the same thing as the real horse . . ." Martin gives a superior smile and says, "I hate horses now . . ." Then he starts doing acrobatics, performing handstands and other tricks almost frantically. Mark and Gloria soon join in and once more the room seems to have been transformed into a huge circus. This continues for about ten minutes. Then Leo comes in. Gloria stops and says, "Look, he is wearing my pyjamas . . . I used to wear them when I was his age . . ." Martin again says, "Let's go and play cards . . ." but no one seems to listen to him. Then he says, "Let's try with Leo . . ." Gloria and Mark now look at him. He whispers "ashtray" in my ear, then concentrates as before. Leo remains there just standing and looks at him, then after a couple of minutes he clearly says "ashtray". (I confess that at this point I am astonished.) Then he points to the ashtray on the table and says, "that ashtray". Now Martin suddenly runs off, Mark follows him and after a minute or two Gloria and Leo also leave.

I remain alone in the room. I examine it more closely and notice that, if possible, Mrs T's collection of *putti* has increased. In addition there are quite a few carved wooden babies, all swaddled, looking like mummies. Most of them are displayed in a baroque cabinet but some hang on the walls where there are also *putti*. There are also three huge, new wooden statues of saints undergoing torture, for instance St Sebastian; they are over life-size. Near the fireplace I notice two strange looking firedogs, my height and probably made of stucco. The rest of the room is more or less the same with its heavy curtains and thick carpets.

After about five minutes I hear Gloria and Martin on the other side of the room. Martin says, "Let's play hide and seek . . ." but soon runs off again. Then Gloria comes in followed by Leo who is holding a small balloon. Gloria tries to grab it but Leo resists. He says he wants to burst it and tries to do so by poking at it with his fingers. Gloria says, "No, let's not play with it . . ." but he seems determined to burst it – with no success. After a few minutes Martin comes in silently and Leo doesn't realise that he is there. Martin goes behind Leo and starts making faces, pretending to be a monster-vampire attacking him. He seems quite serious while doing this and his expression is not a teasing one. Leo suddenly realises that someone is behind him and he looks very frightened, then tries to run away but Martin trips him up and he falls down. He lets go of the balloon and Gloria immediately snatches it. Then Leo runs away followed by the still silent and serious-looking Martin. Gloria plays a bit with the balloon, throwing it to the ceiling and she asks me again about Italy. Is Milan nice? Are there many parks? Did I know some English before coming to England? Then we hear Leo and Martin on the other side of the room and Gloria joins them. After a couple of minutes I decide to do likewise. As I approach I see Martin holding a kind of bronze trident such as Poseidon carries. He is near Leo and he starts teasing him with it saying, "This is how one should treat a baby . . . this is how children should be treated . . ." and once again while doing and saying this his expression is quite serious, I would almost say absorbed, as if following some kind of representation of his own. When he notices me his attacks become more make-believe. I think he has somehow perceived that I was going to stop him. Leo is holding a plastic bag filled with air and now Martin snatches it and starts poking holes in it until it is completely deflated. Then he drops it. He goes up to an old prayer-stool and starts trying to poke holes in it with the trident, not in make believe but in earnest. Gloria intervenes almost immediately (I was also going to do so) saying, "No, don't . . . what are you doing?" Martin looks astonished and also a little frightened then he says, "But I heard people say that holes mean that it is old . . . I was trying to make it older . . . older furniture is more valuable . . ." and he really seems to mean what he is saying. Gloria says, "Yes, but not those kind of holes . . . only those made by wood-worm . . ." again Martin looks taken aback. Then Gloria takes away the trident and he releases it without resistance. She says, "This trident belongs to the statue of Poseidon that is in the other room . . . I'll take it back."

Mrs T now comes back (all this time she has been talking on the phone, probably in her room where from time to time I had heard her laughing loudly). She says, "Forgive me Sandra . . . you know it was a friend of mine . . . I hadn't heard from her for ages . . . and she had to tell me the whole story of her life . . . you know, all the important things . . ." and while saying this she goes to the other end of the room and sits on the sofa where we were sitting before. I follow her. For a while she looks blank and totally lost in thought. Gloria now returns holding Leo's balloon and she starts throwing it up to the ceiling but cannot reach it. I hear her saying, "I just want to reach it . . ." Suddenly Mrs T seems to wake up and says, "Stop it, Gloria . . . you can't reach the ceiling . . ."

Then Mrs T turns to me and starts talking. She says, "Gloria is such a child . . . she is still a child . . . but in other respects she is very mature . . . probably much more mature than her age . . . but then it comes out somewhere else . . . it is always like that . . . if you are more mature in one way . . . the childishness comes out elsewhere . . ." The telephone rings and she goes to answer it. She starts talking about where to go for Christmas, whether to rent a house, how much it would cost, etc. but I am not listening very carefully to what she is saying as I feel a little embarrassed, particularly when the topic changes to men. She goes on talking for about ten minutes. Gloria continues playing with the balloon until her mother says, "Gloria, here's your father" (her first husband) "on the phone for you . . ." She says goodbye and Gloria now speaks. It is getting late but I have the impression that Mrs T wants to talk to me so I decide to stay a few minutes longer. Martin, Leo and Mark now come in and they all start doing acrobatics together. Mrs T says, "Leo is very fond of Martin . . . he follows him everywhere . . . and Martin is very good with him . . . you know, often they even sleep together in the same bed . . . sometimes Martin prefers to sleep on the floor . . . you know, he sort of prepares a tent for himself and sleeps in it . . . and Leo follows him into it . . . you know I allow them to have some fun . . . once in a while . . . especially as at last they are willing to sell us some more rooms downstairs . . . so Martin will have his own room . . . at present he sleeps with Mark . . ." I notice that Martin slips silently behind Leo putting on the vampire or monster act, then he goes back to acrobatics. Mrs T looks lost in thought for a moment, then says, "I have to keep a watch on him quite a lot" (she is still speaking about Martin), "I cannot always allow him to sleep in the tent as he has to wake up very early . . . he goes to school a whole hour earlier . . . you know, with all the retarded children . . . a teacher supervises them . . . you know she tells me he steals . . . from time to time . . . I am worried about him." I ask her whether she has taken him to see anyone, a specialist. But she looks blank. After a while she says, "I am worried about him . . . his teacher too . . . she is afraid that he may deteriorate . . . he even steals from Mark . . . but it isn't possible to do without any instruction . . . or education . . . he is kind to his friends . . . but you know it is just a façade . . . he doesn't learn . . . and with us he can be really vicious . . . yet he is attached to me . . . just imagine, he once told me, 'I am your son after all' . . . but he doesn't learn . . . he tries to be clever and he is a boaster . . . but it's all a façade . . . he is empty . . ." I have the impression that Martin, although uninterruptedly going on with his acrobatics is listening to all this although all the while his movements become more and more frenetic. I again tell Mrs T that if she is worried about him she should ask for an outside opinion and help. I say that I will give her my new phone number so that she can phone me if she needs any help of that sort. She doesn't seem to listen to the first part of what I am saying and then she says, "Thank you, I will write down your number in case I meet someone who might need it . . ." She takes her address book and writes my number in it. I say that I have to go. She becomes blank and remains sitting there a while; then she stand up and goes to the cloakroom. On the way she asks, "And how is your son? Do you still have just the one son?" I ask her about her husband and she says, "He is well . . . my father is not well . . . he is eighty-three . . . he suffers from some kind of cerebral swelling . . . you know he forgets . . . he is often completely absent-minded . . . you know he doesn't understand . . ." I say that I am sorry about that. She says, "But you know he is old . . . I still collect old furniture on the other hand . . . you know there was an article on my collection in House and Garden . . . and what is your work now?" I reply "psychoanalyst", but I am sure that she is not listening although she says, "I'll phone you if I need anything . . ." We return to the sitting-room and I notice that Martin is still tormenting Leo, poking his fingers into his face. All three boys are in a heap on the floor. Mrs T says, "Say goodbye to Sandra . . ." and they all wave at me. Then she takes me to the door and says smilingly, though rather absent-mindedly, "Good-bye Sandra . . . thank you for coming . . ." and I thank her too.

In this observation Mrs T's remarks on Martin's total failure at school, on his incapacity to learn, remember, pay attention, probably need no comment. His capacity to form symbols also seems patchy, as his brother Mark clearly describes when he says, "If he saw an illustration of a horse he would try to ride it . . . he just couldn't distinguish . . . the illustration to him is the same as the horse." The same incapacity is to be seen in the episode where he pokes holes in the prayer-stool, firmly convinced that any hole automatically confers age. His mother also mentions this incapacity to distinguish and to act accordingly, as in his stealing, his cruelty, etc. His resorting to tricks and deceit is now proving to be pathetically ineffective. The non-stop acrobatics probably protect him from total collapse and from the crushing feeling of inadequacy and failure. We see the same thing again when he engages non-stop in jumping and other acrobatics after listening apparently unperturbed to his mother's tragic and cruel comments on him. His restless seeking of friends, his intense social activity, his search for exciting contacts and alliances, as when laughing with Gloria, all seem to have the same protective, pseudo life-giving function. But both excitement and activity do not appear to prove very effective. Often Martin will suddenly look deflated. He seems, at some point, to realise the pointlessness of his search for heights – as he shows when, after scaling the baroque wardrobe he declares, "It is empty up here . . ." Underneath his muscular armour and his responsive surface, aloofness, insensibility and slyness are all still clearly present: the façade hides a secret, desperate world.

Although his hair now seems normal I have, on the other hand, the impression of witnessing an even clearer, more extensive loss of his capacities, if not of his total self. While it is difficult to know what to make of such extraordinary items as the supernumerary row of teeth or the extrasensory perception and paranormal faculties, the world in which Martin now moves and lives certainly seems a rather distant, alien and primitive one – as is seen in his great readiness to retreat immediately into darkness after spying on me at the beginning of the observation. Martin's world seems to be a solitary, mindless one where no learning, memory or absorption exist. In it children are seized by monsters and drawn back to a primitive sensation-based universe of darkness and of purely physical expressions and movements. In it babies are treated cruelly and are tormented and not allowed to live autonomously or to come out of their narrow, womb-like tent. Their potential and capacity for mental and emotional life is sucked dry and further development meets with an unnatural barricade. All of this, I believe, is clearly reflected in Martin's cruel treatment of his younger brother Leo and in his saying, "This is how one should treat a baby . . . this is how children should be treated . . ." Similarly there is the way in which he attracts Leo to live and sleep with him in his 'tent', and in which he follows him like a vampire, making him stumble and fall. It is noteworthy that this, of course, was just the kind of cruel treatment to which Martin was subjected as a baby not so very long ago.

Nor for that matter does he seem to be treated with much humanity or consideration in the final observation. In his primitive, womb-like 'tent', communication doesn't seem to be a verbal, face-to-face human one; other mysterious, perhaps animal channels, like 'contagion' or emanation seem to be used instead. By this, however, I do not mean to suggest that Martin necessarily possesses real extrasensory powers or paranormal qualities. It may all just be a trick. But beyond the 'trick', whatever this may be, the fact remains that this kind of indirect, non-verbal, invasive form of communication seems congenial, even if not ideal, to him. With it he seems to regain control and access into other people's minds – when they are deaf to him on the normal plane.

In retrospect, it strikes me that Martin doesn't seem to be content any longer to live alone and undisturbed in his primitive, solitary world. He tries now to attract proselytes and followers, seducing others to live and move as he does. The other children, in fact, just follow his seductive propaganda of a life with no conflicts, no needs and no pain, a little like the rats and the children in the story of the Pied Piper. The result aimed at would seem to be a suicidal leap into a primitive, almost animal-like existence where mindlessness and emotional deadness are dominant. The kind of influence he exerts over his siblings is, for instance, clearly revealed in the scene where he begins to resort to a non-stop, trance-like movement which seems to transform the darkness of the huge sitting-room into an immense circus tent. The same quality is no doubt to be seen in the magnetic, almost hypnotic attraction he is said to exert on his numerous friends.

With this gloomy account Martin's story now comes to an end as this was my last observation. Unfortunately I do not hold out much hope for his improvement in the future, nor do I feel much optimism that his mother will eventually listen to the advice that treatment should be sought for him.

II

Jack

[I observed Jack regularly for about one year. Then, as the family moved to an even more remote district, I kept in contact with them on a once-a-term basis until Jack was four years old.]

The background of Mrs G and her family could hardly have been more different from that of Mrs T for they lived on the outskirts of London – a poor, gloomy, working-class area, densely populated by Irish immigrants – in a small, overcrowded, poorly lit, semi-detached brick house. Mrs G had been a maid before setting up her large family. The flat was extremely sparsely furnished. For friends Mrs G relied on her neighbours, a crowd of chattering Irish women who would drop in to compare notes on the latest price of cabbages, sprouts, turnips, carrots and so on. This observation was accordingly far less colourful and eventful than the first one. But the monotony and drabness were not just due to the setting, for they were in fact characteristics, and important ones, of this particular family, as I hope will emerge from my account.

My contact with Mrs G was established through her family GP who gave me her name, phone number and the probable date of the birth of the baby. He told me that she would expect a phone call from me a couple of weeks before the delivery, due in about two months. However, something went wrong, for when I rang Mrs G to arrange for an appointment she sounded surprised and perhaps also a little annoyed and said that the baby was already about a month old. Not having heard from me for such a long time she thought that I had forgotten, or changed my mind or something. Then without asking me any further questions and without more ado she arranged an appointment for the following week.

After having spoken with her on the phone I realised that not only did she assume that I knew about the child's premature birth, but also that I already knew a lot about both her and the baby. In fact all that I knew, and this came from her doctor, was that she was in her early thirties and that she already had three daughters aged ten, eight and five. Therefore when I went to see her for the first time I did not even know the baby's name or sex or date of birth.

I found out his name and sex during my first visit but it took me quite a while to find out the date of his birth and during the whole of my contact with Mrs G I never heard anything more about the delivery and only once did she mention her pregnancy. So even now I know nothing about the premature birth. Unlike Mrs T for whom birth was to be a nightmarish process to be forgotten at all costs, for Mrs G it was seen as a non-event, something that was never felt to have taken place at all. Before describing my first impressions of her at any length I propose reporting in detail an account of our first meeting so that readers can form their own impressions more or less at first hand.

Observation One

I ring the bell and Mrs G immediately comes to open the door. She is holding the baby in her arms. She says hello to me without smiling and asks me to come in. She opens the door of the sitting-room, asks me to sit down and then says, "Forgive me a moment . . . I still have to finish changing him . . ." and she goes out. I sit on the sofa. I haven't yet been able to see much of him but I do notice that he is quite tiny; he is wearing a kind of smock and a nappy; his legs are uncovered. He has had hiccups since I came in.

Mrs G is somewhat masculine in appearance, sturdy, muscular, not tall; she has short hair and is not particularly attractive; she wears trousers. She remains in the other room for about five minutes and in the meantime I examine the sitting-room. I notice a sofa, an armchair, a baby bouncer, a cradle and an open fireplace. In another part of the room there are a few chairs and a table; nappies and pyjamas are hung up everywhere. There are lots of pictures on the wall – of Mrs G's wedding, of her other children and many of religious subjects – of the Madonna, Jesus and of various saints.

After some five minutes Mrs G returns. She is holding the baby with one hand while with the other she holds his nappy and pyjamas. The baby still has hiccups and is now wearing just a smock; I see that he is a boy. She lays him across her knee, rather far from her body. As she puts him down his hiccuping stops but his arms and legs start trembling and after a minute his chin starts to tremble as well. He looks up at the ceiling and apart from the trembling he makes no other movement. She puts his nappy on, then his pyjamas. He continues to tremble and look up at the ceiling. Then, when she has finished dressing him, she sits him up, supporting his head and with one side against her stomach. His arms and legs immediately stop trembling and he keeps his arms at his sides, but his chin is still trembling. He looks fixedly in front of him and doesn't move at all. She looks at him (up to this moment she has been talking to me) and notices that his chin is trembling and she says, "But what's the matter with you?" He looks into her eyes, his chin trembling only a little; then she puts her hands on his stomach and starts to rub it. Immediately the trembling stops. He doesn't move but keeps his eyes turned to his mother and looks straight into her eyes. He keeps his arms at his sides, with the fingers slightly open. He doesn't move either his legs or his feet and he stays like that for quite a long time.

His mother talks to me while still supporting his head and she goes on rubbing his stomach with her hand. She asks me a lot of questions but I notice that most of the time she looks lost in thought and that her eyes are very blank. To begin with she asks me what my work is and why I wish to observe a baby. I say that I am working with a group of children and that I thought that it would be a good idea to observe a baby. She asks, "How old are the children?" I reply that they are quite young. She looks abstracted and says, "Yes . . . I see . . . and where are you from?" I reply that I am Italian and she now looks at me and smiles and asks me what part of Italy I come from. I say Milan. She says, "It must be terrible for you, this horrible weather . . ." I say that Milan is in the north so that the weather is more or less the same as in London. She smiles at me and says, "And you have got a nice big umbrella . . . but is it true that women in Italy cannot go out freely alone? . . . A friend of mine was in Italy for a while . . . I don't remember where she was . . . in a small town . . . and she said that the women there could only stay indoors . . . not go out . . . mainly in the evenings they have to stay shut up . . ." I say that in some parts of Italy it is still like that but not usually in the larger cities. She looks lost in thought then says, "Lots of beautiful clothes in Italy . . . and shoes as well . . . are they very expensive? . . . because it is terribly expensive to buy anything Italian in England . . ." I say that Italian goods are much cheaper if you buy them in Italy (but she doesn't seem to be listening to me). She says, "And why did you move to England?" I say because of work. She says, "Oh, I see, so you are married . . . have you got any children?" I say that I have one child and she asks me if it is a boy or a girl and how old it is. I say that he is a boy and nine years old. She says, "I see . . . so he is quite big . . . he" (she looks at the baby) "is a boy too . . . so he is very special (she looks at him and smiles) . . . the girls are at school now . . . so I can look after him . . . and he is also special because with the girls I was much busier and I had to look after all of them . . . he is a good boy . . . he was born a month ago . . . he sleeps very well during the night . . . so your child is quite big now . . . did he go to nursery school?" I say yes and she says, "My elder daughter also went to one for a while but she didn't like it . . . so after a while she stayed at home and I didn't send her any more." She asks me where I live and I say near Finchley Road. She asks me if my son goes to school near there and I say yes.

Then she asks me his name and I say Filippo. She says, "A nice name . . ." and says that her child is called Jack. Then she says that she knows Hampstead very well as she used to work in that area as a daily help before the children were born. She asks me where I go shopping and I mention Sainsbury's and John Barnes. She smiles and says, "Yes, they are very good . . . not very expensive . . . but do you sometimes go shopping in the centre as well . . . like Oxford Street?" I say that I do not particularly like going there as it is very crowded and I get tired. She smiles at me and says, "I too don't like it . . . my feet swell . . . and my back starts to ache . . . after a while I just feel like taking my shoes off . . . it is better to go to Brent Cross." Then she asks me if I go back to Italy for the holidays and I say yes. She says that she too will be going back to Ireland in the summer. She is Irish, as is her husband and they have been living in London for fifteen years; her mother still lives in Ireland. Then she looks at the baby and says, "He will be bigger by then . . . he is so tiny now . . . it is difficult to find clothes for babies when they are so small . . . everything is too big for him now . . . pants are quite a problem because they are so big so that all his wee comes from everywhere and he gets so wet . . . then it is a problem with this weather because I keep washing his nappies but they never get dry . . ." She now looks at him (he has not moved during all this time) and she says, "But now I think that you can go down in your chair a moment . . ." and she puts him down in his baby bouncer.

To begin with, the bouncer is turned away from me so that I can only see that he is moving his arms a little in a sort of circular movement but then she turns him to face me. He moves his arms in the same sort of way, not far from his body; then, almost immediately, he starts moving his head as well. His legs are still and his hands are open. He stays like that for a couple of minutes, then he stops moving altogether, with his arms at his sides, moving only his eyes which roll almost continuously. This goes on for a few minutes until he turns his head slightly against his shoulder and he touches his sweater with his mouth; from time to time he makes a slight sucking movement. While doing this he stares at something, at first quite intently but then more and more blankly, and he starts to dribble a little. His mother notices that he is dribbling (in the meantime she had continued to ask me questions) and says, "Hey . . . what are you doing? You don't want to eat your sweater", and she picks him up. She sits him on her lap facing her and I can see that his legs and arms are trembling. She puts him with his stomach against her breast and immediately he stops trembling. Then she puts him over her shoulder and starts patting his back. He doesn't move. She says, "He loves that . . . he could go on like that all day . . . and this is also the best way to get him to sleep . . . I couldn't do this with the other children . . . I was too busy . . ."

Then she goes on talking to me, though still looking abstracted. She goes on mechanically patting his back and if she stops even for a second he immediately raises his head, turns his face towards her and stares at her intently. Every time she smiles back at him and says, "Come on . . . you know that you have to close your eyes and go to sleep . . ." She asks me, "Are you not going to have other children?" I say, "We'll see". Then she asks me at what age children teethe; I say that Filippo cut his first tooth when he was about eight months old but that I think it varies. She certainly has quite a lot of experience herself having had three other children. She says, "Oh, I thought you were a nurse . . ." I say that I am not a nurse. She smiles at me and says, "Because when I was in hospital there were two girls training as nurses and they were doing more or less the same thing as you . . . but only in hospital . . . I will have to go to the hospital to get some food for him today . . . it is much cheaper there . . ." Then she says that all her children were quite slow in teething and walking. She asks me if Filippo goes swimming and I say he does. Then she asks me where he learnt to swim and I say that he learnt it in Italy as it is easy there, with the sea quite near. Then she asks me how I manage when Filippo is on holiday, for instance at half-term. She says that if I like I can bring him with me. I say that usually I try to arrange things with other mothers so that we help each other and so that the children can be with their friends. She asks me again if I would like to bring him and I reply that if he has the opportunity of being with his friends I don't think he would want to come with me. I say it is just the same when I have to go out shopping. She laughs and says, "Yes, I see what you mean . . . it is the same with my daughters . . ." Then she says to Jack, "But now I will have to put you down . . ."

She stands up and puts him in his cradle, on his stomach. He turns his head in my direction and brings his hands near his face. He keeps his eyes wide open and stares in front of him. She wraps him in his sheet and then goes out of the room remaining out for about ten minutes. To begin with he doesn't move at all. He keeps his hands near his face, again with the fingers slightly apart. He moves his feet a lot. After a while he starts to touch his sheet lightly with the thumb and the index finger of the right hand. He stops moving his eyes and stares in front of him even more blankly. From time to time he half closes his eyes. Then his mother returns. She goes near the cradle and says laughing, "His eyes are still open . . ." Jack starts frowning and moving his eyes again and then makes a sort of whimpering sound. She says, "I know what to do . . ." and she puts a little teddy bear under one of the legs of the cradle and starts rocking it. Jack stops whimpering and frowning and starts touching his sheet, again with the same two fingers. He half closes his eyes and stares rather blankly.

His mother goes out for a moment and he closes his eyes and seems to sleep.

Then she returns and asks me when I will come next. She says that for her this day and time are fine. I say they are all right for me too. Then I say I should like to come once a week for about an hour. She says that is quite all right for her. Then, pointing at Jack, she says, "And you had better behave properly . . . otherwise this nice lady won't come and see you any more . . ." Then she asks me if I would like to see him having his bath or if I would rather see him being fed. I say I would like to see him awake but that otherwise she shouldn't worry and should just carry on with what she usually does. She says, "Today I gave him his bottle just before you came . . . he was hungry." Then I say that I have to go and she takes me to the door and asks me if it was difficult to get to her and which way I came. I say that I came by car and it only took me about ten minutes. She says, "I hope you can find a place to park . . . sometimes it is very difficult . . . as all the men put their cars in the street." Then she shakes hands with me and says, "See you next week then . . ."

What is impossible to grasp in reading just the one observation is the sense of monotony, immutability and immobility that characterised this and each subsequent contact with Mrs G. This first observation, apart from a few irrelevant details, could have been any other observation, for week after week after week Mrs G went on repeating more or less the same things and asking more or less the same questions. Nearly every time she asked me things like: where did I go shopping? Was it in Brent Cross or in John Barnes? Had I ever been to Oxford Street? Was I going back to Italy for the holidays? And was Filippo at school? Only changes in the weather and of the seasons introduced slight natural changes in the monotonous flow of her conversation. In the winter she would ask me things like: was the heating already on in my house? Had I already put antifreeze in my car? During the summer she asked: had I already put away those lovely woollies which she seemed to imagine my mother was continually knitting for me, or was I now able to hang the washing outside? For the rest she went on asking the same questions and I went on giving more or less the same answers to which, in any case, she did not seem to listen, looking totally lost in thought, staring blankly the while, with her eyes and mind miles away. In a sense she, like Mrs T, simply went on and on, each time mechanically wrapping herself up in an endless stream of words which flowed automatically from one topic to the next, and often at the same time she would be equally mechanically patting the baby's back; she would go on for hours on end, always in the same monotonous tone of voice, like some long, repetitious lullaby.

The link between her phrases and her words was purely conventional, that is based on their sound, and she attached one word to the next mechanically. As was shown, for instance, in the first observation when she said, "Because when I was in hospital there were two girls there training as nurses and they were doing more or less the same thing as you . . . but only in hospital . . . I will have to go to the hospital to get some food for him today . . ." Where it was the sound of the word "hospital" that led on to the next item, like a chain. As with Mrs T it was very difficult to pick up any deeper or more logical connection in the endless stream of words. Sometimes the content of her phases seemed to express fears or anxieties, yet her voice, even when talking about, say, a terrible accident or the Christmas holidays or the cold weather, always had the same expressionless, monotonous quality and her eyes the same vacant look. Her non-stop talking, like her constant questioning, did not seem to have the function of communicating or of asking something. It seemed, rather, to have the function of wrapping her almost physically in an impenetrable and immutable membrane or safety net of words. In fact she only seemed to feel safe if such a net was impenetrable and absolutely familiar, hence her constant repetition of the same questions and the same words day after day.

More often than not Mrs G would answer her own questions even before I had the chance to say anything. As, for instance, in the first observation when her immediate response to my saying that I was in England for work was, "Oh, so you are married", as if she could not even consider the possibility that it might have been my own work. Frequently she would question me about Filippo or myself, then immediately, as if shutting off my answer, she would say, "Like the girls . . ." or, "Like myself . . ." or, "The girls are the same . . ." Therefore she never really asked any real questions and was quite satisfied by my smiling and only answering "yes".

In fact at the beginning of our contact I sometimes answered in a more complete, detailed kind of way, as in the first observation. But I soon realized that this was far from being reassuring and satisfactory to her. Like Mrs T, she did not want to know more; in fact any new added detail opened up for her new unknown possibilities and non-similarities between the two of us, all of which posed a threat to the boundaries of her safe, well-known, limited world. Again like Mrs T, she was trying to mould me in a cloudy reassuring way around herself. All similarities reassured her; all differences had to be wiped away either by not seeing them or not listening to them, or else dealt with by building around them a kind of safety net of possible explanations in harmony with herself and with her own tightly-bounded world.

In the first observation I think she was relieved to learn that I was Italian: Italian women lived immured indoors. Also, for her Italy meant the Catholic religion, Rome and the Pope and therefore a strong religious link was possible with Irish people like her. Catholicism was seen as one of our chief equalisers. She never for a moment doubted, not even when on occasion faced with my ignorance, that I could have been other than a practising Catholic. It did not take me very long to realise that she had built up an image of me that was entirely shaped by her own fantasies about my life. Needless to say, such an image had little or no resemblance to my real life. She transformed me into an aspirant nurse, temporarily working in a private nursery school run by a terrible headmistress who was also a nun. She married me to a young doctor with a practice near John Barnes and she endowed me with a fabulous mother who was always knitting for me, and with a kind *au pair* girl who helped me with the cleaning day and night. But most peculiarly my name was changed into an improbable "Mrs Passi" which was to remain unchanged as long as I knew her.

As time passed it became apparent to me that, through her constant stream of words and seeming bombardment of questions, she was trying to fend off some primitive 'pre-verbal' fear of becoming detached from a flat, well-known adherent object and of being pushed out into an unknown, vast, multi-dimensional world. Her conversations sounded more and more like monologues through which she was trying to make us completely adhere to each other, rubbing off all the differences and gluing herself to me, or rather, to a limited, flat, narrow version of me. Her questioning now had a 'seeking to adhere' quality and was apparently aimed at desiring to know all the details of my life so as to be able to adhere to each of them. But in order to keep up such an illusion of total adhesion and fusion her questions had to be repetitive and designed to elicit predictable answers. She always wanted to know the same details, ignoring all the rest of my life 'unknown' to her. Although her image of me was inevitably constructed on the basis of very superficial similarities and very few details, nevertheless a total adhesion and equality seemed in a sense vital to her. Any other possibility was felt as a rejection, or abandonment of a terrible kind; if we were not identical and closely adhering, acting and thinking as 'one soul', she felt put down and completely lost. For instance, when I made the mistake of saying that I would not take my son with me at half-term, she plainly immediately felt 'put down' and, acting this out in reality, put Jack down. Then, a moment later, she walked out 'dropping' both Jack and me.

By transforming me into Mrs Passi, the aspirant nurse, the gap between us was closed and I became on a par with her peer group neighbours, perhaps a little more adventurous but no more than that. With me, as with all her friends, she maintained an affectionate and warm relationship such as one might have with a family pet dog or cat, or a favourite teddy bear, or a cosy blanket. The type of contact that she had with me was well represented by what she called "your lovely fur coat". This fur was in fact well-worn and somewhat shabby and she doubtless suspected that it was only rabbit or civet, but nevertheless she never stopped praising it, telling me how much Jack loved it and that it was the thing that Jack best remembered about me. Each time I left she approached holding Jack and would say something like, "Touch her lovely fur coat . . . feel it . . . your nice friend is wearing her lovely fur coat . . ." or, as she once said, "Never mind if it *is* old . . . I'd even like to sleep in it . . . you must even wear it in summer, Mrs Passi . . . you'll have to wear it all the time . . ."

In saying this she was, I believe, telling me that she was clinging to a long-standing ideal, for her but by now also for Jack – that of being wrapped up "all the time" in some kind of warm, "lovely", protective object with which she could have a continuous, wrapping sensuous contact. Such an object protected her from the cold, from novelties, from everything, and also provided her with everything, as it were constantly, without ever a break and with no need for her to have to ask for anything. She thought that I possessed such qualities and as time passed I began to realize that for her I acquired the 'ideal' texture of a warm, soft, teddy bear-like wrapping object. She also thought that I possessed a kind of mythical, ideal mother in Italy, knitting warm "woollies for me all the time", or cooking or looking after me. In her fantasy my mother was always available to me, twenty-four hours a day, ready to carry me anywhere. As she once asked me, "And your mother, does she drive you around all the time? . . . will you be staying with her all the time?" Not surprisingly, being given such a mother I was also in her fantasy able to provide a baby with a constant 'blissful' protection "all the time". Once she said to Jack, "You should visit Mrs Passi during the holidays . . . she could take you around in the pram all the time . . . you are lucky . . . I would also like to be a baby and have a mother looking after me all the time . . . and taking me out in the pram as well." Obviously such a mother had nothing much to do with me or my own mother or with any real mother 'outside'. Such an 'ideal' had to do more with someone carrying you around "all the time", in a state of being physically contained and physically linked to mother, like being inside a womb.

Such a condition represented for Mrs G an ideal kind of mythical 'Paradise Lost' which she was trying to recreate at all costs and with all possible means. Her constant wrapping of herself in a stream of monotonous words; her way of placing any image out of focus, staring blankly ahead until she probably lost sight of the outside world; her almost constant occupation of performing mechanical actions and of carrying on almost equally mechanical monologues; her hours spent in front of the television screen in a state of total mindlessness;

her seeking of a cutaneous, almost totally undifferentiated contact with people. These were, I believe, the means she employed to try to recreate such a state.

Each observation was obsessively ritualized. Each time she greeted me with a remark about the weather; then she asked, "And Filippo, how is he? . . . is he at school?" Then she brought in some tea and biscuits; each time the ritual allowed little or no variation. This applied also to her daily routine activities: rising, breakfast, shopping, cleaning were always performed in the same fashion in the same order and at the same time. All these duties and rituals were carried out mechanically, mindlessly and almost automatically, with her eyes staring blankly and her mind being equally blank. Many of her actions and conversations were imbued with a bemused, almost self-hypnotic quality, as when she went on patting Jack's back for hours on end, or when she repeated the same remarks and questions over and over again. Through her endless repetition and ritualization she seemed to be trying to render everything around her immutable, predictable and as constant as possible, like some membrane. Her space was penetrated almost only by regular, predictable 'beats' and by familiar sounds; in such a space no unusual sights were to be seen, no different tastes or smells or temperatures experienced. Her sleepiness also created a safe, protective kind of barrier against the novelties, stimuli and changes in the outside world. Everything outside this space simply lost focus, differences were blurred and everything was seen as in a daze or through a haze. In this state she achieved a kind of fusion or adhesion with her environment and with the people living in it; she created a sleepy, timeless continuum and a dormant world where differences were blurred, where novelties were almost absent and where other people seemed like pale shadows adhering to herself.

Wrapped as she was in all her safety nets or membranes, she appeared to me as a gentle and fragile creature, but at the same time undifferentiated and quite primitive. When she sat passively and limply staring into space I had the feeling that I was observing a kind of amorphous mass, pulsating and following an impersonal biological clock, her monotonous talking being the only visible movement. But even that had a rather reflex 'muscular' or 'beat-like' quality. Her uninflected words, pronounced at regular intervals, sounded like a simple reflex activity, an involuntary action that just kept her going and alive. My presence, like any human presence, served merely as an incidental stimulus to set such activity in motion. When in such a state she seemed quite unable to react personally or individually to the impingement or the stimuli of her environment. Her reactions seemed automatic, taking the form of withdrawal or closing up, as response to an unwelcome stimulus. Alternatively she would seem to be turning towards, absorbing and opening her pores to a source of energy that could filter in – activities that required no thought and which even simple organisms like plants could automatically perform.

She seemed to live in an even more primitive, almost primeval state than did Mrs T. With Mrs T one had the impression of watching a foetus moving restlessly inside the womb, whereas with Mrs G it seemed that one was observing something much more embryonic than that. Her passivity was striking; unlike Mrs T with her continuous, aimless physical movement, Mrs G was immobile. The more sophisticated sensations, like excitement, were consistently absent and she seemed only capable of feeling the simpler sensations, such as warmth or cold. Her solitary monologues, with their regular rhythmic quality, did not even have the strength of proper evacuations, such as would require an already functioning excretory system; they were at best automatic discharges. Her boundaries were not defined or contained but were shapeless, amorphous, fluid and plastic. When we sat together on the settee she seemed to be glued to me rather than seated next to me. When engaged in monotonously patting Jack's back she seemed to be fused with him and he merely an extension of her. When one of the neighbours dropped in she absorbed in a spongelike fashion the talk of prices and just re-echoed them, with maybe some colourless comment about freshness, or the like. Most of the time one had the impression that she amalgamated to and fused herself with her environment. Not only did she seem to lack well-defined external boundaries and an efficiently filtering skin, but she also gave the impression that there was an almost complete absence of any cohesive structure within, such as a nucleus or a core or a backbone. In this way she was reminiscent of a viscous, non-differentiated creature like an amoeba rather than of, say, a baby with its well-defined appearance, great complexity and often sharply delineated personality. She reminded me of an ovum fused with its own matrix, or of a gelatinous embryo in an early stage of development, rather than of a foetus with its progressively differentiating growth, capacity to move and to react, and so on. She also seemed to lack the more crustacean, armour-like quality of young Martin, or the surface vitality of Mrs T. When she sat blankly staring out of the window, or wrapped herself up in a monotonous stream of uniform, uninflected verbal commonplaces, her capacity for abstract thought did not seem to be much further developed than that of Dumbo, her cat, which lay for hours voluptuously stretching or sleeping in front of the fire.

Her lack of memory was equally striking, as evidenced by her asking me the same questions over and over again during the same observation. Her power of fantasy or imagination was also embryonic, if not non-existent; she seemed unable to explore mentally beyond very limited and narrow horizons, again like her cat which did not seem to be able to move beyond the constricting streets and courtyards of the gloomy neighbourhood.

Not surprisingly Mrs G's contact with Jack was also rather primitive, epidermic, sensuous and animal, although mostly I had the impression of there being no contact at all, as if he were non-existent or not yet born for her. Even animal warmth was in fact a rarity in their minimal interchange. Most of the time Jack was kept at a distance, almost out of reach and out of sight, left to sleep in his cot or left alone for hours in his bouncer and later on in his play-pen. Even when present Mrs G was mostly absent-minded and vacant-looking. One had the impression that although they were together in the same room they belonged to two totally separate and distinct worlds, with Mrs G staring blankly into space and Jack motionless or silently engaged in one of the limited range of his solitary activities. Even when Mrs G picked him up she mostly kept him at a distance, laying him across her knees, far away from her body, as if he were merely a peripheral appendix. Whenever she held him close to her body it was mainly to pat him mechanically and endlessly for hours, with his face over her shoulder staring at the wall, without her ever looking at him or talking with him. On the rare occasions when she did speak to him she usually merely repeated one of her favourite phrases like, "look at the birdies", or "clap handies", or "I'll get you". Only occasionally were they face to face, their eyes rarely met and then just for a very short time. Mrs G would usually go blank again or resume her monotonous patting while saying things like, "Come on, you know you have to close your eyes and go to sleep . . ." as we saw in the first observation. I had the impression that she almost never saw him or perceived him as a separate human being.

On the other hand Jack, with his passivity and immobility never acted or reacted as an individual. When Mrs G was patting his back or holding him at a distance on her lap, it seemed to me that their contact was not very different from the time when he was still in her womb when they were physically linked but had not yet seen one another. At such moments I had the impression that Jack still belonged to his mother's body, as if still living inside it without having yet found a separate place and space inside her mind. Later on, when Jack had difficulty in falling asleep and had increased the range of his physical movements, she would immediately place him in his bouncer, or later on in his play-pen encouraging him each time to move and bounce so as to, as she herself said, "keep himself company". But unfortunately even in his muscular development Jack was rather backward and slow, as Mrs G used sadly to announce during many later observations, saying things like, "He's not yet crawling", or "Not walking yet", or later still, "He's not talking yet."

Yet at times she could also watch and observe accurately and perceptively Jack's feelings, needs and states of mind, but she simply registered them, commented upon them and then sat there passively staring blankly into space. Her perceptiveness and sensitivity had a rather primitive, animal quality as if she could perceive with secret antennae or through the pores of her skin. In this way, too, she reminded me of her cat who could sense at a distance and immediately perceive through some mysterious channel of communication when the environment was safe and that it was therefore safe to lie undisturbed in front of the fire.

Probably, from what I know of her history, Mrs G had never met anyone who could help her to progress further than a primitive, animal-like mindless state of unawareness. Her childhood had been a long chain of sorrow, misfortunes and deprivations. She was the fifth of seven children and her father died when she was only four leaving the family in great poverty. Her mother was always terribly depressed, two of her brothers became alcoholics. Her elder brother, "the only support of the family" was obliged to emigrate to Australia to find work so that he could send money back home. I am sure that the list of unhappy events was longer than this but she only once told me about her past and this was related in her usual flat, resigned tone of voice, as if she felt that this was all that could be expected from life. Yet in our relationship I was struck how, although slowly and laboriously, she was able to use my receptive presence to take the initiative to learn new skills. For instance, after many lessons she learnt to drive and she declared that it was after having seen me drive that she had thought for the first time that perhaps she could learn something that would have been quite unthinkable before. At the beginning of our acquaintance she used to wait for me just hunched up on her settee. After a few months she began to stand in front of the window looking out to the street waiting eagerly for my car, "your mini" as she called it, to appear on the horizon and she would admiringly watch my clumsy efforts at parking it. She reminded me of a small baby watching for its mother from behind the bars of its cot and smiling with joy when she appeared in sight. Like a baby, given appropriate 'tutoring' she was able to learn to move and walk. Passing her driving test was in a way a concrete, tangible proof of her having been able to 'move forwards' and make progress.

But apart from learning how to drive, I had the impression, particularly towards the end of our contact, that she was beginning to use my presence to start thinking and reflecting; she was becoming aware of Jack's condition and of the feelings that such a condition elicited from her. As she told me, looking tearful (and I was too) after the very last observation, "Goodbye, Mrs Passi . . . it's been nice knowing you . . . you have helped me you know . . ." Unfortunately by that time four years had already elapsed and Jack had by then been left untreated overly long. Probably it would still have taken Mrs G a long time to act on my suggestion of seeking help for him.

Before going on to Jack, however, I. would like briefly to describe the other members of the family – the three girls and their father. It will perforce be a short account as I saw them only rarely: the girls on occasions such as half-terms or the school holidays or the Queen's Silver Jubilee, and their father twice when he was at home from work. It would seem that Jack too saw them very infrequently, at least compared with the amount of time that he spent with his mother. His father usually left for work very early and came home very late, and he often had to be away for days, if not for weeks, working on some site outside London. His sisters also went off to school early and came back around five. Then, from what I was told, they were busy with their homework, had an early supper and went to bed. The three sisters, Katie, Mary and Bernadette, were respectively ten, eight and five at the time of Jack's birth.

Katie

Katie was a sweet, gentle, timid creature, as plump and shapeless as a sack of potatoes and as short-sighted as a mole. She was always kind and sweet to her mother, to me and to everyone else, and was very attentive and maternal to Jack. In fact, from what I saw, she was more of a mother to him than was his real mother. She picked him up and held him close to her, she spoke with him, she knew his tastes and needs, and gave him the toys that he liked. She also somehow knew what was 'wrong' with him. As she once said (see Observation Two) pointing at Jack who was dribbling and staring blankly into space, "But where are you? . . . You are far away . . . I think that you are in outer space . . . you are not in this world . . . you must belong to another world, somewhere like the moon . . ." But she herself, although perceptive and warm, was rather 'short-sighted' and, according to her mother, was unintelligent, incapable of learning, and was a failure at school. She also told me that Katie had no friends. She would often say of her such things as, "Katie, she is very good at sewing . . . you know she is very good at every kind of housework . . . she just doesn't like school or studying . . . she loves cooking . . . and looking after Jack . . . or the other children too . . . she loves being at home . . ." Even going shopping was too much of an enterprise for her and the much more adventurous Mary usually had to accompany her. One could picture her carrying on the same sort of life as her mother for ever, staying inside her shell all the while. Apparently her ideal, too, was that of being wrapped up in my fur coat, as her mother once told me (see Observation Two) when she was taking me to the

door. "Your lovely fur coat . . . you know that Katie also likes it a lot
. . . she said that she would like to have a pillow like that . . . and take
it to bed with her . . ." Like her mother, I doubt whether she could
give Jack more than a kind of tender, 'animal' warmth. When in her
arms he certainly seemed to warm up, at least when he was small. But
later on I never noticed any sign of any kind of dialogue between
them, their interchange seemed to remain purely physical with Jack
immediately curling up in her lap the moment she came near him.
During the last two years of my contact with the family I did not see
Katie again and I do not know whether in the end he refused this kind
of contact with her as well. His mother by then used to say that he was
refusing contact with everybody so I suspect that this may also have
included his sister Katie.

Mary

Mary, his second sister, was quite different in character and probably
the brightest of the family as well as the most independent. She
certainly was the only one to show a more venturesome spirit and a
desire to leave the narrow streets of their gloomy neighbourhood. Her
eyes were big, blue and sparkling. She was, according to her mother
"no problem at school". She was also "talkative" and "not in the least
shy", with plenty of friends; she was "full of initiative" and showed
clear individual tastes of her own. But perhaps her brightness, independence and individuality also represented a threat to the security of
her mother who would often say, smilingly, things like, "She really is
a problem . . . with her clothes . . . she just wants to wear what she
wants . . . with Katie it's different . . . she wears anything . . ." Her
difference from the rest of the family also probably represented a
threat to the others as evidenced from one of Mrs G's remarks: "Is
Filippo going to try for a scholarship? . . . Mary could too . . . but I
don't want . . . you know . . . I thought that this would make her too
different from the others . . . you see I think it's not fair . . . with a
scholarship we could afford a private school . . . but you see it would
not be fair . . ."

Mary's interest in Jack was only marginal. Busy as she usually was
she only glanced at him from time to time, occasionally dropped some
witty remark about him and moved quickly away intent on some
other interest of her own. I doubt whether her presence was anything
other than a brief gleam of light for him. Her sparkle and brightness
often seemed to have a rather manic, effervescent quality, and she was
busy running about and joking all the time. Mary was more forthcom-
ing with, and interested in me than were the rest of the family; she
asked questions about Florence and Venice, and about school and life
in Italy. She also told me that her dream was to belong to the fire

brigade, or to become a beautician, or chiropodist or something in that field. Given her manic temperament and her state of constant excitement, I am somewhat doubtful about her potential for eventually making any of her dreams materialise. On the last occasion that I saw her, when I went to see the G's briefly to say goodbye before I left, she had transformed herself from a tomboy into a caricature of a *femme fatale* copied from a cheap magazine, with high heels, long hair, long pendant earrings, a plunging low-necked T-shirt and a 'revealing' skirt with a deep lateral vent.

Bernadette

Bernadette, the youngest, was somewhat frail but certainly not gentle, at least as far as Jack was concerned. She probably would have liked to have been the 'baby', if not the only child in the family. All her efforts were directed at capturing her mother's attention and at frightening and tormenting Jack whenever she got the chance. Her mother was an easy victim: a little insistence was enough to cause her to move her vacant eyes away from Jack. In order to avoid a blank response, Bernadette would generally try to engage her mother in some game or task such as asking her to draw something or to read a story. Any opportunity served to frighten and torment Jack: as soon as her mother left the room, or even as soon as her eyes went blank, Mary would make loud noises, pinch his chin, violently shake the bars of his cot to which he was clinging. Each time Jack was visibly frightened. Later on I was told that Jack followed her like a shadow, imitating whatever she did. I never personally witnessed this as in the latter part of my observation I did not have the chance to see them together so that I could not tell whether in the end Jack became a blind, ardent follower of his main tormentor, as did young Martin with his sister Gloria. Bernadette frequently acted the 'baby' with me, trying to copy Jack, so that she would move around sucking from his bottle, or would lie on the carpet kicking her arms and legs. At other times she would try to draw my attention away from him by asking me questions or showing me something. Then, if all else failed, she would sit in front of him or she would stand in a position calculated to make it impossible for me to observe properly. She could not bear my looking at him and ignoring her.

Mr G

Jack's father I only saw twice. The first time he was in great pain, probably from a slipped disc. I was told that he worked as a builder and therefore had to carry great weights. He was very tall, fair-haired, with big blue eyes and was quite attractive, like the hero in a movie.

But his look was somewhat vacant and he had the appearance of an alcoholic. On the first occasion I thought that this expression might perhaps have been due to the drugs that he had been given to relieve the pain. The second time that I saw him he was very kind but he still looked somewhat vacant. When Mrs G once remarked that all Irishmen drank heavily and were often alcoholics, I remember thinking that her husband too could have come into this category, at least judging from his appearance. But this remained just a suspicion as Mrs G very rarely spoke about him.

Mr G possessed the same gentle and warm quality as his wife. He seemed to behave kindly to Jack and would look smilingly at him before going off to work. Later on his wife told me more than once that "Daddy is not a baby man . . ." Each time that she spoke of him, in connection with his work or his sporting activities in Ireland, it was in a tone of 'due respect' or else she would look at me smilingly, with an air of complicity as if to say, "We both know what men are like . . ." This made me wonder at times if perhaps she treated Jack differently from the girls, following some kind of traditional ideal of masculinity. In my last observation she also apparently wondered about this as when she remarked, "But I cannot understand why he is like that . . . could it be because he is a boy and the others are girls?" Was his mother more distant and less cuddly with him? Did she demand less of him and treat him with more respect? Did she feel that his being a boy made him too different from her? She certainly encouraged his independence, his muscular strength and probably a kind of toughness also, while at the same time speaking of him with a mixture of pride and admiration. I often heard her say things like, "Boys don't cry.", or "You are a man . . . no cuddling for a man.", or "Princess Anne had a boy . . . boys are very special." And in the first observation she remarked, "He is a boy too . . . so he is very special . . . the other three are girls . . ." However, not having seen her with her girls when they were babies nor knowing what kind of babies they were, these speculations must just remain questions; and it must also remain a problem why it was that Jack was the only one of the family to retreat completely and hostilely from the world.

Jack – the first six months

Jack was not born with a 'shell' – at least from what I was able to observe. Unlike Martin who seemed to show right from the start a painful difficulty in opening up to the world, Jack, for months before withdrawing, showed a great tenacity in holding on to anything that could help him to emerge. But he seemed from the outset to be frail and no fighter. He was born some twenty days prematurely and although I was never told his birthweight he was certainly underweight. With his tiny features and delicate bones he looked like someone too weak and naked to support the light without the protective covering of the womb. This was evident also in his readiness to "fall to pieces" or "fall apart", to quote his mother's strikingly appropriate words. Each time that he was left unsupported he would begin to rotate his arms and legs and head, and one had the impression that at least for a short time this movement helped to hold him 'together'. But this did not last, for after a few minutes he would begin to tremble; first his arms and legs, then his trunk, then his chin and finally his lips, and soon he was shaking all over as if with fever or with intense cold. In a trice all the separate parts of his body seemed to become completely 'unstrung', and then minutely fragmented with each small part affected by its own independent tremor. Unless his mother intervened at this stage his 'dissolution' seemed total and akin to death – he would thereupon cease to tremble and would stop all movement. He would lie passive and motionless dribbling the while from his open, inert mouth. Watching him I had the impression of seeing his life trickling slowly and irresistibly away. His eyes seemed to undergo similar transitions for, when left to himself, he would first fix them on some object, often something bright like the light, almost 'pinning' his eyes on it. For a moment this stratagem appeared to work; at least his eyes seemed to have anchored to or hooked onto the object. The rotary movement, both of his eyes and of his limbs, would momentarily bind together each part but it was always a moment of rest only, for then once more the limbs would begin to move continuously and disjointedly, the eyes to roll as if they had lost their anchorage in the ocular orbit. In the end, however, even these movements would cease and Jack would remain immobile, open eyed, glassily and blankly staring. This pattern was first seen in the first observation when Mrs G put him down in the bouncer and he began to move his arms and legs, rotating them. Then his head followed the same movement and his eyes rolled continuously. Yet this movement did not seem to succeed in keeping him 'together'; in the end his blank look reappeared. His attempt to hold on to some object by staring fixedly at it had but a fleeting effect, for once again the blankness and dribbling reappeared. Then came blankness and dissolution; a deathly passivity seemed to be all that remained.

This increasing disintegration, passing from movement to trembling, then to dribbling while at the same time becoming progressively more and more expressionless and blank, was present for months and each time it was like watching Jack die. Probably something inside him died each time as well. Together with the dissolution of his physical links and boundaries I had the impression that I was seeing an even more dramatic dissolution of the thin cohesive nucleus of his fragile ego. Probably in some sense he had come out of his shell too soon, or was born with an over-fragile and not sufficiently developed psychic skin – in the sense in which Mrs Bick uses this term. He was not a fighter. It was very rare to hear him cry or protest, or to see him in any way try to attract someone's attention. Usually his 'drama' took place silently and passively; the sequences just described were never accompanied by even a feeble sound of distress. What was dramatic was his extraordinary capacity to come back to life and quickly recover each time his mother picked him up and held him close to her body, even if not to her mind.

For several months I was able to observe many of these instant 'recoveries', with Jack springing back to life and ceasing to tremble or to engage in continuous disjointed movement. Each time his face brightened and he directed his gaze to his mother's face, following with trepidation even her slightest movements. Certainly no other stimulus, either from within or from outside, nor the use of his limited resources of movement, seemed to have the same 'magnetic' force as did his mother's presence or closeness. No other stimulus had an effect that lasted for more than a few seconds. This was demonstrated in the first observation when his trembling immediately stopped once she brought him closer to her body, or when she began to pat his back and to hold him close to her breast, or as when he looked straight into her eyes as if he knew exactly what it was that he was seeking.

Unfortunately it was only rarely that his mother held him closely, or even looked at him or gave him more than a moment's attention. Yet, at least for those first few months, he showed a tenacity and will to hold on to the slightest sign of attention and had a great capacity to use even seconds of physical proximity to return to life. Then, as the months went by, he unfortunately seemed to lose hope; his eyes stopped looking for human objects and he began to turn more and more often towards inanimate objects. At first he merely reacted to people with indifference but eventually he turned his back on them.

Before closing this account of my contact with Jack I would like to go back to the beginning of it. During the first two months I saw him do little more than tremble, dribble, roll his eyes or lapse into blank-ness. All his efforts at keeping himself 'together' seemed to end in failure. At the same time all his resources and his rare movements were geared to just this end.

On the fifth observation, however, I saw him for the first time with his sister Katie. She was holding him closely in her arms while talking to him. And it was probably no coincidence that on this occasion I noted a different quality in his movements. He was, for instance, holding tightly on to the strap of his bouncer, looking as if he was holding on to the fastened seatbelt of a plane. He did then seem, at least, to have the idea of holding on to something. He did not roll his eyes and was dribbling only slightly. When he was held by Katie in this way he was clenching his fists, whereas previously his fingers had always been spread widely apart. During that observation he gave me the impression of being much more 'compact' and less orbitless. He also cried briefly the moment his mother left the room to go and make tea, and I remember feeling quite relieved as this all felt like a great step forward. In the few weeks that followed, however, I observed almost nothing that was new. Katie was back at school and his dribbling and trembling continued as before.

When he was some three months old, for the first time I saw him being bottle-fed. Whether he had ever been breast-fed remained a mystery as, like his birth, Mrs G never said anything about it. While he was feeding I was struck by the fact that the presence of the teat in his mouth seemed to have a remarkably similar effect on him to that of his mother's closeness to him, or his mother's looking at or giving attention to him. The teat seemed to have the power to pull him together. But during that same feed I also noticed how, in her absent-minded way, Mrs C would automatically move at regular intervals, nearly pulling the teat out of his mouth. The moment it was no longer firmly inside his mouth his eyes went blank, his lips began to tremble, followed by his cheeks, his chin and eventually his whole body.

In this same observation I noticed that Jack was now increasing the range of his movements, particularly when he was left on his own. For instance, the moment that his mother set him down in his bouncer he began moving his feet up and down, then a little later he would begin cycling continuously. His mother also noticed this and said, "He moves a lot during the day . . . his arms and his legs . . . he will become a busy man . . ." While engaged in this kind of continuous, monotonous movement he did not tremble and seemed on the whole to be less inclined to "fall apart".

The following week I observed the only other feed I was to witness. [I often wondered why it was that Mrs G always fed him either before or after I left. The best explanation I could find for this was that to her my visits were in some way like her own 'feeds' and she wished to have as much time and attention as possible from me for herself.] On this occasion Jack seemed remarkably dopey and blank. At times he seemed to focus on his mother, but his eyes almost never met hers as she herself was either blank or occupied in talking to me. Occasionally he seemed to return to life by sucking the teat but, again, his mother kept moving it as she had done in the previous observation. When he finished his feed she gave him his dummy and moved him well away from her breast. Jack immediately went blank and a lot of milk suddenly spilled from his open mouth, as if a plug had been pulled out. In this observation, movement as a means of keeping him 'together' was ever present. For instance, he began moving his head continuously when the feed was interrupted by a phone call; again, he began cycling the moment his mother set him down in his bouncer.

During the observations of the next three months, as his body progressively gained in strength, his movements became more efficient and his trembling stopped completely. As he became more capable of focusing on people and objects his eyes stopped their disorganised rolling movement. However, the dribbling and blankness became even more noticeable and severe. Nevertheless he still seemed to be able to recover his interest in the world the moment that his mother was there with him. He also began to smile the moment he saw her.

Later on in the visit he tentatively began stretching out his arms to her as if asking to be picked up. Unfortunately almost all his efforts to keep her there or to attract her attention were sadly abortive. Each time his hopes seemed to be painfully thwarted and more deeply thrown back on his own resources. In particular his movements became increasingly evident; when not held he would be either stretching or moving his feet up and down, or shaking his head, or cycling. His mother noticed this and several times, while blankly staring at him, she remarked, "Look at you . . . you will become a good cyclist . . ." She was able to notice his activity but not his attempts to initiate some contact with her.

Now that his hands were beginning to exert a firmer grip on things he also started grasping all sorts of objects such as toys, ribbons or straps. Each time that he did so he held on to them desperately as if trying to find anchorage. Later, when he was also able to bring things to his mouth, he never sucked or licked them but instead seemed to use whatever was available as a kind of plug. The moment such an object was removed from his mouth or fell from his hands he began to dribble profusely. He also dribbled a lot of milk. When 'spilling out', his eyes immediately lost focus and his arms went limp; I had the impression that the moment his external anchorage or his concrete plug was removed, he was left completely deflated with nothing inside.

Apparently Jack became very attached to his surroundings especially to the sides of his cot. Mrs G told me, "He feels safe in it . . . he doesn't like any change." When he was about five months old a change actually occurred, for he went back with his family on holiday to Ireland for about a month. This is how Mrs G described this change: "It was terrible during the trip . . . he was bringing back milk all the time . . . I think it was also because he was missing his cradle . . . you know we took the pram with us . . . it is not the same . . . he was used to sleeping in his cradle . . . he can stretch out his arms and touch the sides . . . he has a lot of space . . . I think that he did not like the change . . . and now with this milk . . ." Again I had the impression that once his external surroundings were removed or altered it was as if his skin had been stripped away and he could only lose all his substance. Yet the trip to Ireland was not without its benefits. Mrs G told me on her return, "Everybody liked him . . . he became very spoiled . . . everybody was picking him up all the time . . ."

The attention he received there probably had a beneficial effect, for on the first observation after the holiday when he was about six months old, although his dribbling and blankness were still extremely marked I heard him for the first time utter some sound. This was a kind of "Brr . . ." and his mother correctly assumed that he wanted to express some irritation. In fact he said "Brr" each time that he could not reach some toy. The fact of having received a lot of attention seemed to have rendered him less numb and more able to feel and express emotions. Mrs G too seemed to be more alive. But that was an observation that was altogether more full of hope. The following week his "Brr" had disappeared and I didn't hear it again. Ireland by then was probably a lost memory. Mrs G also soon lost the benefit of the Irish interlude, and back in her solitary routine during the following weeks she became particularly blank and again could give Jack no more than a minute's attention at a time.

Six months to the first year

Around the time that Jack was some six months old it became clear that his development had halted or was even regressing to an earlier and more primitive level. Although up until then I had been aware of his poor development, at that time even the smallest movement and degree of progress were magnified by my wish and hope to see him develop more normally. It was only in retrospect that I was better able to realise the flatness and uniformly monotonous level of his behaviour even during the first six months. However, at least until then he had not seemed to be hopelessly retarded nor was he ever completely so for the first year of his life.

When he was about six months old I noticed a habit of his which I think clearly epitomised the tragedy of his life: he would suck on his dummy, taking the handle and all into his mouth. The moment that his mother pulled it out he immediately went blank and started dribbling profusely as he had done months before. I had the impression that he was desperately trying to retain some object in his mouth, something that he was quite powerless to do with his mother with whom he could only maintain contact for a few fleeting seconds before she removed herself from him. Because of the great speed with which she left him he seemed unable to keep alive inside himself any memory of her; when she was no longer with him he seemed to be empty of everything. The poverty and flatness of his internal world were very evident and at such times his eyes and face lost all expression and life. By taking the whole of the dummy into his mouth I think he was trying desperately to keep it firmly anchored there like a plug. Even the smallest breach was enough to make everything spill outside. But at the same time I had the impression that in his desperate attempt to remain attached to some concrete object he himself remained anchored to a safe but primitive stage of development. In this state he was at one with the object physically, indissolubly linked with it and therefore unable to move even a little way towards the dawn of mental life, towards the beginning of taking in, of introjection and towards the beginning of a purposeful sending out, either through projection or through communication. When fused with the object the distance and differentiation necessary to initiate both introjection and projection, let alone communication, were not present. Physically linked and attached as he was to the object he did not seem to possess any individuality nor even a proper skin; the moment the plug was removed all his contents spilled outside and his life seemed to dissolve.

Jack continued to try to build up a kind of muscular armour, a second skin (in the sense given this term by Mrs Bick), through movement. His repetitive movements seemed to have no purpose other than that. The moment he wrapped himself up, as it were, in obsessive motion nothing, or almost nothing, seemed able to reach him and he appeared to be completely plugged in and shut away from the world. When he was about eight months old I noticed that whilst this movement was carried on he would now often keep his eyes and lips tightly closed. Gradually he ceased to keep his eyes open and continued the movement even when his mother was there talking to and looking at him. Moreover he began looking past people, and his eyes seemed more and more to be attracted by inanimate objects such as the light, the wall and, later on, the television screen. When his gaze was fixed on the light or when he was hypnotised by the television screen, he seemed to be totally immersed in a mindless, trancelike state, and more and more isolated from the world as if he were still living in a secluded, non-mental, womb-like primitive state. All this went hand in hand with the loss of substance.

Jack now was dribbling and bringing back milk most of the time. He seemed to lose all solidity and liveliness, and the poverty of his development became increasingly pronounced. The flatness and monotony of his responses and the infrequency of his attempts at communication were striking. His rare smiles seemed to be merely automatic responses; his very occasional crying always sounded monotonously the same, expressing either a somewhat undifferentiated discomfort or, at times (particularly when Bernadette was there) an equally inchoate panic or fear. Even his muscular progress was irregular and slow. By the time he was ten months old he mostly lay limply motionless appearing to lose even the drive, the energy and the skills to move. It was only slowly, painfully and almost unwillingly that he reached such milestones as being able to sit, crawl and stand up, and he never even seemed pleased by these new skills and used them very little.

When he was a year old he did begin to crawl a little but even when his mother left him outside the play pen he would just remain there holding on to the bars. When he did move this was usually to perform robot-like, automatic and repetitive actions such as rocking his body back and forth for hours on end. But most of the time he would just sit looking flaccid and blank like some wretched, boneless, undifferentiated lump of flesh. Nevertheless until he was a year old or so, there still seemed to be some hope for his improvement for he still seemed capable of springing back to life if only he could be given the opportunity.

In the following observation Jack is eleven months old. His blankness, dribbling and rocking of his body need little comment. But still, when he is given some attention his body suddenly seems to regain its strength. When his sisters play with him he can even laugh and he produces some sounds.

Observation Two

When I arrive I hear a lot of noise coming from the girls inside the house. (I am a little surprised as I had thought that they would have been back at school after half-term.) I ring the bell and Mary comes to open the door. She smiles at me and shouts, "Mrs Passi is here." Bernadette then comes into the passage and she also smiles at me and says, "Mrs Passi is here." Mrs G comes out of the kitchen to greet me and without looking at me she says, "Hello Mrs Passi . . . please do come in . . . they are still home as you can see . . ." Then she preceded me into the sitting-room. (I notice that she looks as if she has been to the hairdresser. She is also wearing quite a lot of eye make-up and lipstick. I had never seen her wearing make-up before.)

We enter the sitting-room and she brings my chair near the fire. Katie is there too; she is sitting on the sofa holding Jack in her arms, quite close to her body but with his face turned away from her. She smiles and says hello. While moving my chair forward Mrs G says, "They should have been back at school . . . but they ran out of oil . . . you know for the heating system . . . I think that it is quite silly . . . they've just had one week for half-term and they should have thought about it then . . ." She then approaches me and says, "Let me take your coat, Mrs Passi . . ." She goes out and remains out a couple of minutes; I can hear her talking to the other two girls, although I cannot hear what she is saying to them. Katie smiles at me and says, "I like your chain a lot."

Jack is holding on to her arm with both hands and is gently rocking back and forth. He stares at me rather blankly. I notice that he is not wearing any socks. Mrs G returns for a second and takes away an empty bottle from the table. Then she comes back and sits in front of me. She looks at Jack and says, "Did you say hello to Mrs Passi? . . . Not yet this morning . . . clap handies for Mrs Passi . . ." He now looks at her but blankly. Then Katie holds both his hands and makes them clap. He smiles momentarily and then looks vacant; then, as she drops his hands he puts his right hand in his mouth. He stares in front of him and just moves his feet backwards and forwards slightly. Katie says, "He can clap hands sometimes . . . but then he loses interest and just puts his hands in his mouth." Then she looks at him and Mrs G looks at him also. Katie says, "But where are you? . . . You are so far away . . . I think you are in outer space . . . you are not in this world . . . you must belong to another world . . . somewhere like the moon." Mrs G smiles. Then she also looks lost in thought and blank like Jack. Katie says, "He's dribbling." I cannot see this.

Now Bernadette and Mary come into the room and they start running round the table which is at the far end. They play table tennis on it and make a lot of noise. Jack looks blankly towards them. He now has both hands in his mouth. Mrs G says, "They went to school on Monday . . . but then they had to come home . . . and yesterday too . . . so today I just rang . . . by tomorrow it should be all right . . ." Then she notices that Mary and Bernadette are removing the table-cloth. She stands up and tells them in a firm voice to put it back and to go and play upstairs. They both leave. She comes and once more sits in her chair. She then says to me, "My brother is coming . . . he should arrive tomorrow . . . he decided to come to London himself . . . I had already arranged with my neighbour that she would come in to help my husband with the children . . . I was going to go but my brother said that it was too complicated for me . . . so he is coming himself . . . I think that he will be here for two weeks before going back to Australia . . . my husband will go and pick him up at the airport."

At this point Jack takes his hands out of his mouth, lets them fall to his side and starts dribbling. He doesn't move. Katie says, "He is dribbling . . . Mummy, can you give me a Kleenex tissue." Mrs G says, "All right . . . let me have him now . . . you go and get his bib from upstairs . . ." and she goes to pick Jack up while Katie goes upstairs. She sits him on her knee, rather far away from her body, facing me. He holds on to her arms with both hands and rocks back and forth. Katie comes back with the bib followed by Bernadette. Mrs G puts the bib on him. He grasps it with both hands. Bernadette goes in front of him (so that at this point I cannot see him) and asks her mother, "What's written on his bib?" Mrs G replies, "Dinner . . . it's not quite time yet . . ." Then she looks at me. "It's very difficult when they are all at home to get organised in the morning . . . he is not dressed properly yet . . . no socks . . . at last we can see your feet . . . it is not very cold today . . ." Then she starts rubbing her nose against his cheek, but he doesn't react at all and just keeps staring blankly.

Bernadette and Mary start playing round the table again, although much less noisily. Katie takes two teddy bears from Jack's play pen and makes them embrace saying, "You see they are hugging, like mother and baby . . . he likes them but what he likes most are those toys that he can put in his mouth." Then she moves the bears in front of his face. He grasps his hands in front of his stomach and looks at them moving his legs slightly back and forth. The telephone rings and Katie goes to answer it. Jack doesn't seem to react. Then Mrs G stands up and goes to the phone keeping Jack in her arms. She talks with a strong Irish accent, and I cannot understand what she is saying. After a couple of minutes she stops speaking, comes back and sits down.

Bernadette immediately goes and stands in front of her, hugs her saying she wants some tea. Mrs G says, "Okay; we'll make some tea for Mrs Passi as well . . . he can go in his play-pen now . . . he still doesn't like it very much . . . he got spoiled with all those nurses around." As she sits Jack in the pen he cries with his mouth wide open, dribbling and closing his eyes tightly. He keeps his arms at his sides but then almost immediately stops crying. Katie gives him a tortoise to hold and he puts its head in his mouth and starts rocking backwards and forwards. Mrs G says, "He has another tooth now . . . it's strange . . . it's not in front . . . it's on the side . . ." Katie points at some marks on the edge of the play pen and says to me, "Look, he made all those marks with his teeth." Mrs G says, "He likes standing up in it and biting it . . . but he's not crawling yet . . . I don't think that he will ever crawl . . . perhaps he will just walk . . ."

Then she goes out followed by Mary and Bernadette. Katie says, "You see, he likes it . . . your tortoise . . . he likes putting it in his mouth . . . your book too. He likes it . . . but what he prefers most is his rabbit . . . because it has longer ears and he can get them into his mouth." Jack now turns the tortoise slightly and tries to put its side into his mouth, then he tries to put the bottom in too. Katie says, "No, the bottom is too big." Then she puts several other toys in front of him and removes a doll, putting it on the table saying, "That is Bernadette's . . . it's not good for him as he might get the hair in his mouth." A kind of square plastic container is also in his play-pen and he now takes this and starts trying to put his mouth on its different sides. Katie says, "But it is too big for you." Then we hear Mrs G calling Katie; she tells her to come and have tea too. Katie goes out.

Jack doesn't seem to notice and keeps on trying to cram the container into his mouth; he is now dribbling a lot. Mrs G comes back with my tea and is carrying a huge slice of apple cake. She sits down, and Bernadette comes in and goes up to her mother and starts hugging her. Mrs G seems a little annoyed and says, "Go and put your jumper on . . . it's not summer yet . . . and you go around without sleeves . . ." Bernadette protests a little; then she goes and gets a jumper and puts it on. A moment later Mrs G stands up and gets a cup of tea and some cake for herself. At this point Jack is still trying to get the container into his mouth.

When his mother returns she sits facing him more directly. He drops his container and stretches out his arms towards the plate with the cake. She says, "But look at you . . . you are dribbling and falling over . . . I know you want some cake . . ." And she starts giving him little bits of apple. Each time he opens his mouth widely and then eats staring intently at the plate. While doing this he holds the bars of the play-pen with both hands. Mrs G says, "I hope the cake is good . . ." I say that it is very good. She asks, "Do you make pastries Mrs Passi?" I reply, "Not much". She says, "I don't either . . . last night my husband was out so I thought I would make some . . . my neighbour, she is fantastic at it . . . but I think you always appreciate more what other people make . . ." She keeps giving more cake to Jack. Then she says, "Eating is no problem with him . . . he eats everything . . . but now the cake is finished . . ." She puts her plate down and I have the impression that Jack tries to raise his body, then he whimpers.

She picks him up and stands him upright on her knees. He starts mechanically to hit at her face while staring at something behind her. Mary and Bernadette come nearer their mother; Katie, too, sits at her mother's feet. Mrs G says, "Katie's hair is a problem . . . it always gets so dirty . . . it's strange at her age . . ." She looks lost in thought for a moment and then says, "I go to my driving lesson today . . . my neighbour will come here to baby-sit . . . it is so expensive . . . I didn't want to miss it . . . I paid for twelve more lessons . . . I hope it will be enough . . ." At this point Bernadette touches Jack and tries to hug him. He draws away from her and Mrs G tells her to stop. I cannot see Jack's face as he is turned with his back to me. Katie says, "He likes the cat very much . . ." Mrs G says, "You know the other day the cat got up on the roof . . . I had to call someone to fetch him down . . . I heard a noise . . . but I thought it was from the garden . . . not from the roof . . ."

Then Bernadette says, "And tell Mrs Passi your dream." Mrs G looks a little embarrassed; then she says, "Yes . . . that same night I had a dream . . . only it was not the cat . . . it was Jack . . . I dreamt that he was trapped in the hole in the garden . . . the one that I thought the cat had been caught in . . ." They all smile.

At this point Jack stops hitting Mrs G's face, he grasps her jumper with both hands and vigorously starts to jump on her lap making a kind of "Grr" noise. They all laugh. Mrs G says, "I think that you are showing off to Mrs Passi . . . aren't you? . . . Look how he is showing off . . ."

Mary tickles his tummy and Bernadette makes faces at him; although I still can't see his face I can hear him laugh. Then Bernadette says that she would like to hold him. Mrs G agrees to this. She tells her to sit on the sofa and gives him to her to hold. She holds him very tightly and he arches himself away from her, rubbing his eyes with both hands and then he starts crying. Mrs G picks him up saying, "Okay, that's enough . . ." He stops crying. She sits down for a moment holding him in her arms. She makes him stand up facing her. He hits at her face while looking at his sisters who are all around him. Then Mrs G puts him down in his play-pen. He grasps the bars looking at Katie who is now moving a doll in front of him.

Katie then announces that she will do a show for Jack. First she moves the doll, then the tortoise and then my book on to the edge of the pen. I can't see him as the girls block the view. I can just see that he has his face turned in Katie's direction. Mrs G looks at me smiling. She says, "He likes having all these nurses around . . . he doesn't like sitting down . . ." She pauses, then asks, "Are you going to be away at Easter or are you just going to be around?" I say that I will be around. She says, "Oh, that is good . . . so you will be able to bring Filippo to the pond with his boat . . . by then the weather should be all right . . ." At this point Jack whimpers but I still can't see him at all.

Mrs G picks him up and stands him on her knees with his face towards her. He stretches his arms towards some pictures on the mantlepiece. She says, "No, you can't have those . . ." Bernadette shows him a small statuette but Katie immediately goes up to her saying, "No, that one is dangerous . . . it's sharp." Mrs G tells Bernadette to put it down. I say that I must go. Mrs G says, "All right Mrs Passi . . . let me go and get your coat . . . your lovely fur coat . . . you know Katie also likes it a lot . . . she says that she would like to have a pillow like that . . . to take with her to bed . . ." Then she asks Katie to go and get my coat, standing beside me (I have got up at this point). She holds Jack with his head over her shoulder. She notices a plaster on one of my fingers and asks, "What happened to your finger? You cut it? . . ." I say yes. She says, "I also did that . . . I burnt my arm the other day, while I was ironing . . ." Katie now gives me the coat and I put it on. Mrs G asks Jack to touch it saying, "Feel Mrs Passi's lovely coat." Then she asks me, "Did you have any trouble getting petrol?" I say no. She says, "Oh, that is good . . ." Then I say goodbye to the girls. Katie says, "You may see us again next week." Mrs G smiles and says, "I hope not . . . I hope you will be back at school . . ." The telephone rings and she goes to answer it. It is her husband giving her a phone number. She writes it down. (Jack is still in her arms but I can't see him.) Then she finishes and returns to me saying, "That was my husband . . . he gave me the phone number where he is . . . just in case my brother arrives . . . so that he can go and pick him up . . ." Then she takes me to the door saying, "Good-bye Mrs Passi . . . see you on Thursday then . . ."

The following years

Our regular contact had by now almost come to an end. When Jack was one year old Mrs G told me that they were going to move to a new and larger house. The following months she was very busy arranging things there and it was also difficult for me to find the time to go and see her in her new, far more distant district. When I finally went (Jack, by then, was some eighteen months old) I was shocked both by her blankness and loneliness, and by Jack's isolation and regressed state. Mrs G sat staring into space and blankly watching the perma-nently switched-on television. In her new neighbourhood there seemed to be no one who dropped in to see her. The houses were few and far between and surrounded by gardens. She had lost all her chattering friends. To pay for the mortgage on the house her husband worked longer hours and was often away. Her daughters attended a much more distant school and by the time they got home it was already dark. I was only able to visit her irregularly as it took me two hours to go and come back. Even Dumbo the cat was no longer there for, disorientated by the change, he had soon been run over. Jack too looked completely withdrawn from the world. He seemed to have gone back to live in a narrow uterine space devoid of people and of any living creatures, a little as in his mother's nightmarish dream. He spent hours curled up like a foetus on the settee, totally impervious to anything or anyone. At other times he would wrap himself up inside the curtains, hidden, silent and immobile. Sometimes when curled up he would grip his penis with both hands in the same desperate grasp as I had seen him use with other objects. I rarely had the impression that he was masturbating, and even when he was the sensuous excitement aroused seemed to create an even more impervious cur-tain between himself and the rest of the world. However, even when not masturbating he didn't seem to notice people and things around him; if anyone or anything entered his field of vision he didn't even blink. He showed no reaction whatever to his mother's talking to him. His expression was empty and dead all the time. Only here and there was it possible to detect some traces of intelligence, but on the whole his mental and emotional life seemed to have been completely aborted and buried. The only word that he would occasionally utter was

"No". His body looked rigid and old, as if it had been mummified; his skin was livid and greyish in hue; he held himself stiffly and walked like an automaton. However, he walked very seldom and moved very little during any of the later observations. He just followed his mother like a shadow at the beginning when we came in and then only occasionally from chair to chair, quickly curling up in each of them. Only from time to time, when holding some inanimate object, would he come to life a little and his mother once told me, "He is mad about cars . . ." The only expression on his usually blank face was hostility and tension. Normally his lips were kept tightly shut; his muscles were tense and he looked out of the corner of his eyes. Not surprisingly, with this tight closure to the world and his desperate attempts to recreate a womb-like, self sufficient world, he tended to eat little and lost quite a lot of weight. At times he seemed openly to hate the outside world, as when throwing bricks at his mother or hurling his car violently into the air. But these were fairly rare occurrences; he usually engaged in little activity and showed very few reactions. A direct observation will best illustrate his condition: Jack is two and a half years old. Since passing her driving test Mrs G asks me each time I visit her to phone her from the tube station and she then comes to pick me up in her huge, second-hand American car.

Observation Three

I arrive around 10.30 and I ring Mrs G from the station. She answers the phone and says, "Hello Mrs Passi . . . just wait there . . . I will be with you in five minutes." I wait outside the station and run to the car as it is raining quite heavily. She opens the door from the inside and greets me saying, "Hello Mrs Passi . . . nasty weather today . . . how are you Mrs Passi?" I reply that I am well and she immediately asks, "And Philip, how is he? . . . is he at school?" I say yes. She says, "The girls had their half-term at the end of October" (we were then at the end of November). "Now they are at school also . . . and your husband how is he?" I say that he is well. I ask about her family and she says, "All are well . . ." I look at Jack; he is strapped into his little seat at the back of the car. He looks taller. He doesn't move at all. His expression is a little blank and at the same time almost hostile. He gives me half a glance, then turns his head slightly sideways and stares blankly out of the window, without moving and keeping his arms at his sides. Mrs G looks at me while I am looking at him and I say that he seems to have grown. She suddenly brakes as a car almost bumps into us. (I think that probably she was distracted as she was looking at me.) She says, "Oh, dear . . ." Then after a short pause she says, "It will soon be Christmas . . . and the New Year . . . is Philip changing school next year?" I say that he will be changing in two years' time. She asks if I have thought about the next school and, "Are you sending him to a private school?" I say that this is likely but that I do not yet know which school will take him. She asks, "Has the headmaster given you any advice? . . . you know private schools are better . . . there are fewer children . . ." (Again another car comes very close and almost bumps into us.) She asks, "And what about your car? . . . your Mini . . . is it still going?" I say yes. She asks, "Have you already put some antifreeze in?" I say yes. She says, "I have to . . . the weather is cold . . . I don't like this kind of weather . . . when it rains . . . I'd rather have it colder, but not raining like this . . . more like it is in January . . . it is cold . . . but then the winter is almost over . . ." Then she looks completely lost in thought and keeps on driving. I look at Jack again for a moment and again he turns his head away. She notices that I am looking at him and says, "He can talk now . . ." We arrive at the house. She stops the car and looks at Jack saying, "Aren't you going to say hello to Mrs Passi?" He turns his head away, closing his lips tightly and looking out of the window, without moving. She says, "He gets all shy . . ." She gets out of the car and undoes his straps. She says, "It is terrible . . . so muddy . . . your shoes get so dirty . . . he never wants to wear shoes . . . he always wants to keep his slippers on . . . because there is Batman on them . . ." She shows me his slippers which have Batman on their toes. She picks them up and quickly goes indoors carrying him. I notice that he looks very stiff. As she enters she puts him down and says to him, "Will you say hello to Mrs Passi now? . . . no . . . he gets all shy . . ." He stands near her and looks down at his feet, keeping his lips tightly closed and his arms at his side. She shows me a plant on the table and says, "Do you remember it? . . . you see it is doing very well . . ." and she smiles without looking at me. (I brought her the plant some while ago.) As she takes Jack's coat off she says, "Now you'll show Mrs Passi some of your cars, won't you? . . ." He doesn't react in any way. I say that I have brought him a little car and I give it to her with a small box of chocolates. She says, "Oh, but you shouldn't Mrs Passi . . . you come all this way . . . and it is expensive . . . you shouldn't . . ." Then she opens the door of the sitting-room and asks me to take a chair. She puts the box of chocolates down on a cupboard and switches the electric fire on. She asks me, "Is the heating on yet in your house?" I say yes. She says, "Oh, that is nice . . . it is nice to have the heating on now . . . in the morning when you wake up . . ." Then she sits on the sofa. Jack goes near her. He lies on the sofa curled up in the foetal position leaning his head against her side. He stares blankly in front, still without moving. She shows him the car but he just gives it a glance, then continues to stare blankly, still without moving. She says, "It's not nice of you . . . Mrs Passi has

come all this way to see you . . . and you.don't even say hello . . . or
talk to her . . . or look at her present . . . all right . . . I'll give it to
Bernadette . . . she will like it . . . all right we'll give it to her . . ."
Jack stands up and goes and lies down in the other armchair. He
curls up in the foetal position and almost hides his face against the
back of the sofa (actually I cannot see his face at all). He remains
there without moving. Mrs G repeats a couple of times that she will
give the car to Bernadette, then she looks more and more lost in
thought and stares out of the window. After a while she again looks
at him. She stands in front of him and starts pushing the car towards
him saying, "I'll get you . . . I'll get you . . ." But from what I can
see he doesn't react at all. If anything he seems to be withdrawing
slightly but I cannot be sure as she is covering him with her body.
She sits back on the sofa and, looking out of the window, says, "He
cut that chair once . . . on its arm . . . with a pair of scissors . . . I was
out . . . he was here with the girls . . . they just left the scissors out
. . . now I have banned the scissors . . . you know I was out . . . the
girls are out now . . ." (she pauses at this point and looks very blank)
"they are at school . . . they had half-term at the end of October . . .
Bernadette and Mary go together . . . it takes a long time to get there
. . . you know they walk and talk . . . I tell them, 'You could wake up
much later, at eight, instead of seven fifteen if only you would walk
faster', but they like it . . . but in the evenings I get worried . . . if
they are not home at a certain time." She pauses and looks lost in
thought, then asks, "And Philip, does he walk home alone?" I say
yes. She says, "Katie comes home alone too . . . she takes a bus, it's
easier for her . . ." Again she looks lost in thought, then she says,
"She finds it easier now at her new school . . . she is in the lower
stream . . . she finds it easier to be there . . . she is not a bright child
. . . in the other there were some bright children . . . she finds it
difficult when she does not know something . . . she didn't know
most of what she was expected to know . . . this school is easier . . ."
She is lost in thought and then asks me, "And Philip, does he do a
lot of sport at school?" I say yes. She says, "Does he like it?" I say
yes. She says, "Katie too, she likes it . . . but she gets cold . . . Philip
will do more next year . . . but she gets cold . . . you know they go
out in this weather in just a short-sleeved jumper . . . she doesn't like
that in this cold . . ." She looks out of the window and says, "It is so
cold now . . . the garden doesn't look nice . . . I should do something
about the roses . . ." Then once more she looks lost in thought. After
a while she looks at Jack. He is still curled up like a foetus in the arm
chair. She goes closer to him pushing the car towards him a couple
of times and making car noises. He doesn't respond at all. She says,
"I will tell Daddy tonight . . . it is not nice what you are doing . . .
Mrs Passi having come all this way . . . I will tell Daddy . . . some-

times he gets all shy, even with his father . . . and then there is this man who lives next door . . . he likes him . . . he sees him all the time . . . but even with him some days he goes all funny . . . he just doesn't pay any attention to him . . . he just hides . . . and ignores him . . ." She again tries pushing the car in his direction but with no success. She stands up. After a moment Jack too stands up, then he goes and lies on the sofa again in the foetal position. He is facing me but he doesn't look at me at all. I notice that now he keeps his hands in his trousers and I have the impression that he is holding his penis, or at any rate his underpants, very tightly. She looks at him and then sits near him a moment saying, "He is dry now." (She looks at me at that moment while most of the time she has not done so.) Once more she looks out of the window and says, "It was after the summer . . . when we were away he was still wearing his nappy . . . but when we came back his bottom got sore . . . I don't know why . . . not because of not changing his nappies . . . I changed him often . . . but he got sore . . . so he gave it up . . . probably it hurt him . . . and now he is completely dry . . . first thing in the morning he goes to the toilet . . . before tea . . ." Again she looks lost in thought then she says, "I will make some tea now . . . you will talk to Mrs Passi . . . you will keep up the conversation . . . it will be a rather one-sided conversation I am afraid . . ." Then she goes out.

Jack doesn't seem to react to her going. He remains on the sofa with his hands on his penis and without moving until his mother comes back (after about ten minutes). Mostly he stares in front rather blankly, but now I notice that from time to time he gives me a quick glance, but as he meets my eyes he turns his own away and half closes them for a moment. I try to talk to him but he doesn't respond. Then his mother returns. She gives me a cup of tea and two sandwiches saying, "I put in one spoon of sugar . . . is that right Mrs Passi? . . . I wasn't sure . . . no cake this time . . ." She goes out again and comes back with a cup of tea and a sandwich for herself and with some biscuits and a plastic cup of tea for Jack. She shows him the cup but he doesn't react at all. She puts his cup down on the small table saying, "I will have to tell Daddy . . . when he comes home . . . Mrs Passi will not come to see you any more if you behave like that . . ." She takes the car and pushes it a couple of times in the direction of his face but he still doesn't respond or even blink. Then she actually rolls it over his cheek and on his head. He half smiles momentarily but without looking at her.

Then she sits down and starts drinking her tea. She again says, "Have your tea . . ." and this time he says "No" in a determined, rather gruff voice. Then he stands up and goes and curls up in the other chair as before, keeping his face out of sight. He remains like that, without moving, for quite a while, still holding his penis with both hands. Mrs G asks me, "Do the children have lunch at your nursery?" I say yes. "And do they have a rest after lunch?" I say yes. "In the nursery near where we used to live they have little beds . . . Do you remember Mary? . . . the little girl who lived next door . . . in the other house . . . now she goes to that nursery . . ." She looks lost in thought for a moment then, looking at me she says, "He will go there later . . . he still talks too little . . . I can understand him . . . but it would be different for the teacher . . . and with other children". (While saying this her eyes go blank again.) "I don't know . . ." After a while she asks me, "Do you think that he has grown?" I say that he looks much taller than last time. She says, "His hair is cut short . . . like a boy . . . he is fair . . . I like his hair shorter . . . your hair is different Mrs Passi . . . I like your new cut . . . you look much younger . . . it suits you . . . I don't like changes . . . hairdressers just go mad . . . and cut it too much . . ." She remains silent for quite a while, staring blankly into space while drinking her tea and eating the sandwiches.

Then she stands up, takes my cup and says, "I'll make you another cup, Mrs Passi . . ." I thank her and she remains out a few minutes. Then she returns with the tea and sits down again. She asks me, "Have you already started your Christmas shopping, Mrs Passi?" I say not yet. She asks, "Have you thought yet what present you'll get for Philip this year?" I say I haven't thought about it yet as it is difficult to think of something that he'd like. She says, "Yes, it is difficult . . . you can't give him toys any more . . . you gave him a bike last year" (she looks lost in thought). "Mary and Katie will get a bike this year . . . Bernadette will get a doll . . . so that is easy . . . and with him anything will do . . . but has Philip got one of those games you play on television?" I say no. She asks, "Does Philip have friends?" I say yes. She says, "Oh, then that is a good game . . . he can play it when his friends come . . . they can play together . . . my neighbour has three boys and they bought one last Christmas . . . and they play a lot with it . . ." I say that this seems a very good idea. She asks, "And where do you go shopping Mrs Passi?" I say that I mainly go to Sainsbury's and John Barnes. She says "Yes, I know them . . . I also go to Sainsbury's . . . is there a food store in John Barnes?" I say yes. She asks, "And do you sometimes go to Brent Cross as well?" I say yes. She says, "I like it too . . . you just go in and you have everything there . . ." Then she asks, "And do you ever go to Oxford Street?" I say very rarely. She says, "Me too, too many people there . . . I saw in the paper that they already have all the Christmas decorations up . . ." She looks lost in thought and then asks me, "Will you go back to Italy at Christmas?" I say yes. She says, "Yes, your husband is his own boss . . . so you are able to take ten days off . . ." She ponders and then says, "Will you stay with your Mother?" I say yes. She asks, "Is your mother well?" I say yes. She smiles and asks, "Is she still knitting those nice woollies for you?" I say that I hope so. She smiles and asks, "Is wool expensive in Italy?" I say that it is more or less the same price as it is in England. She says, "Real wool is much better. I also like to have knitted things for the girls . . . those you buy are synthetic . . . they get all baggy . . . better to spend a little more but get good quality . . . his trousers are good quality" (she points at Jack who is still in the same position and hasn't moved at all) ". . . they were Bernadette's trousers first . . . then I was going to send them to my sister in Ireland . . . but luckily I didn't . . . he has another pair handed down from Bernadette . . ." Again she looks lost in thought, then she says, "I was in Ireland for the summer . . . but when did I last see you?" I say it was just before the summer. I ask her how her mother is. She says, "She is well . . . her blood pressure is all right now . . . but you know she is still very upset because of my niece . . . you know the one that was run over . . . she can't recover from that." (Before the summer holidays she had told me that her niece had had an accident. She was paralysed and on a ventilator.) "You know that she is still in hospital, on a ventilator all the time. They tried to take her off for a while . . . but then she got a chest infection so that she had to go back on it . . . my mother, she just can't get over it, in hospital all her life . . ." She looks lost in thought for a while, then she asks me, "And will you have some training in hospital as a nurse as well?" I say that I don't know yet. She says, "My neighbour, she has four children . . . but she has always wanted to become a nurse . . . you know that it was her dream all her life . . . and now that the children are older she has started to train as a nurse . . . she says that she will try to study in the evenings . . . taking it gradually . . . but she has her mother helping her . . . so that is a help." She pauses then asks, "And do you have someone helping you Mrs Passi?" I say that I have a daily help. She says, "Oh, that's good Mrs Passi . . . but then you have to prepare dinner . . . cook in the evenings, and the nursery as well . . . there is no finish to house work." She stands up to offer me the plate of biscuits, then she says, "But do take another . . . you have come all this way . . ." She sits down again, takes a biscuit herself and while eating it she asks, "Is your nursery far from Finchley Road Station?" I say no. She says, "I haven't yet been on the Jubilee Line . . . then you get out at Finchley Road Station . . . did you leave your car near the station?" I say yes. She says, "Oh, that is good . . . and do you have far to go with the car?" I say not really. She asks, "Is it still going well, your car . . . your Mini . . ." I say yes. She asks, "Have you put in the anti-freeze yet?" I say yes. She says, "It is better, with this weather, . . . so cold and wet . . . my washing never dries . . . do you have a tumble-drier?" I say yes. At this point Jack stands up and comes and lies near her on the sofa, still in the foetal position. He keeps both his hands between his legs and doesn't move at all. His eyes are half-closed and he looks very blank. She says, "He is in a bad mood today . . . with this weather . . . one of those days . . . you can't do much about it . . . perhaps he is sleepy as well . . . show your cars to Mrs Passi, will you?" He doesn't react at all. She says, "He likes Bernadette . . . he follows her everywhere . . . like her shadow . . . when she comes home she takes him . . . they go under the stairs and she plays with him . . ."

She looks at Jack while he nibbles his biscuit, and says, "Do you think that he is skinny? . . . he doesn't vomit or anything . . . but I think he is skinny . . ." While saying this she gently touches his tummy. He raises his right arm and covers his face with it. She says, "He is just blocking off . . . when he blocks off he doesn't even blink if you talk to him . . . he is very good at blocking off. . . ." Then she looks quite blank herself for a while. She asks me, "And do you celebrate Christmas a lot in Italy, Mrs Passi?" I say yes. She asks, "And do you celebrate it on Christmas Day?" I say yes. She says, "Of course, I forgot . . . it's a Catholic country . . ." She looks lost in thought a while, then looking directly at me and smiling she asks, "Have you seen the Pope on television? . . . I mean when he went to Ireland . . ." I say yes. She continues to smile and says, "That was really nice . . . my brother-in-law was there . . . he went to the Mass . . . he was close . . . you know there were so many people . . . some were quite far away . . . so they did not see much . . . but he was quite close . . . I saw it on TV . . . it was a week-end . . . my husband was working in this place outside London . . . and we were there too for the week-end . . . I looked at television . . . this Pope travels a lot . . . I thought he was going to come to England after Ireland, but he didn't . . . he went to the States . . . and he has been to Poland . . . and to Mexico . . . he is a nice Pope . . . also the other one, what was his name . . . John 23rd, he was a nice Pope . . . I didn't like Paul 6th, he wasn't very nice . . ." She looks lost in thought, then she asks me, "Have you been to Rome?" I say yes. She says, "Have you been inside St Peter's?" I say yes. She asks, "Is it always so full of people?" I say that it is always rather crowded, and particularly when the Pope is giving an address. She asks, "Do all your sisters live in Milan?" I say yes. She says, "So you will see them . . . I go and see my sister-in-law . . . you know in the other place . . . once a week . . . you know I also meet my friends there . . . they don't drive . . . while I do . . . so I can go . . ." Jack now stands up and goes near the small table. I notice that he touches the plastic cup. She says, "Have you written to your friends for Christmas?" I say not yet. She says, "I must also write to the States . . ." I say that I have to go. She says, "All right, Mrs Passi . . . just give me a ring whenever you want to come back . . . you know that I am always here . . . so that you can phone me any time . . ." I notice that Jack has spilled his tea. She says, "Oh, he has spilled his tea . . ." She touches his trousers and says, "They are wet . . . forgive me for a moment, but I will have to change him . . ." She picks him up and I hear her going upstairs. While she is out I hear her talking to him. She says, "Where is Bernadette?" He repeats the name 'Bernadette'. Then she says, "Now I've got to change you . . ." and he repeats the word 'change'. She comes back with him. He is holding himself very stiffly in her arms. She sits him on her knee facing me and tries to put his jumper on. He closes his lips tightly and resists her with his arms. She says, "Come on . . . otherwise you will have to stay here . . . we'll leave you here . . . I'll go with Mrs Passi . . . do you want to come with us?" He says "No" in a very gruff voice. She finally succeeds in putting his jumper on. She stands him down to put his slippers on and says, "We'll have to buy some new ones soon . . . you can't even tell it's Batman any more . . . we'll have to buy you boots . . . like Mrs Passi . . . nice boots, Mrs Passi . . ." He again says "No" and she repeats, "We'll leave you here then." She puts his coat on. I too put mine on while she says, "Look at Mrs Passi . . . you remember her . . . perhaps you should have worn your nice fur coat Mrs Passi . . . you remember her nice fur coat Jack? You liked it very much . . ." She puts her coat on, then says to me, "You can phone me . . . I am here all the time Mrs Passi . . . you know that you can always come . . ."

Then she picks Jack up, closes the door and we go out. She opens the door of the car for me, then she straps Jack into his small seat at the back and gets in herself. She starts driving and asks me, "At what time do you have to be back home in the evening?" I say that usually I am back around five o'clock. She asks, "Is there a lot of traffic when you come home?" I say yes. I notice that she is making rather a long detour in order to get back to the main road. She says, "I do this because it is dangerous . . . the road is so full of traffic . . . so I don't want to turn the car there . . . I prefer to go all this way . . . at least there is no traffic . . ." She points out some shops to me saying, "You see, the shops are very nearby . . . you know in case I forget something . . . and that is my doctor's house . . . it is very convenient . . . you don't even need a car . . ." She drives looking rather lost in thought, then says, "Sainsbury's is further away . . . I need the car for that . . . but they have a large car park . . . so that I can put it in there . . . it is convenient . . ." She pauses again, looking lost in thought and then adds, "It is convenient to drive a car . . . you remember I took the driving test at about this time last year . . . so many lessons . . . but it is convenient . . . you know now with the girls . . . they also go to music lessons . . . I couldn't do that without the car. Mary also wants to go to French lessons . . ." She pauses and then asks, "And Philip, does he speak Italian as well as he speaks English?" I say yes. She asks, "Does he find it confusing?" I say no. She says, "That is lucky . . ." We are now near the tube-station and she stops the car and opens the door for me. I say goodbye to Jack but he doesn't even look at me. He keeps his lips tightly closed and stares blankly out of the window. He holds on to his seat with both hands. Mrs G says, "You must promise that next time you will talk to Mrs Passi . . . otherwise she will never come back again . . ." Then she says goodbye to me. "I hope you will have a very nice Christmas, Mrs Passi . . . if I don't see you before . . ." I thank her and wish her and her family a happy Christmas too.

What seems tragic about this observation is not only Jack's obvious state of retreat but also Mrs G's almost total unawareness of it. Her obliviousness continued for at least another year during which time whenever I saw Jack he was curled up like a foetus. Then towards the end of our contact Mrs G did seem to come alive somewhat to his plight and during one of my last visits she spoke quite tearfully about him. Jack, as usual, was being very difficult and withdrawn. He kept his lips tightly closed and never looked at his mother or me. When we came in he was walking like an automaton. Screaming, he refused to take off his coat, his gloves and his bonnet, and Mrs G told me that he insisted on wearing them all the time, like some life-supporting space suit. He threw away the books and the cup she offered him and stood rigidly and stiffly in front of the television with his eyes glued to it. His expression was either completely blank, or, when his mother interfered, hostile. He didn't seem to hear what she was saying to him and appeared to be isolated inside a tight impermeable space of his own. When she looked at him Mrs G seemed both hurt and worried. She told me that music and the feel of soft, furry objects were the only things he liked. "He likes his tiger . . . and the furry feel of it . . . he likes touching things . . . you know the feeling of the texture . . . the girls the other day went out and bought him a tiny little scrap of mink . . . and he loved the feeling of it . . . he was always touching it . . ."

Later, in between talking about my coat, John Barnes and Oxford Street, she told me, "He is difficult . . . he is different from the girls . . . he doesn't learn . . . he cannot remember . . . he doesn't listen . . . he doesn't even recognize his father . . . the girls get all excited when he comes home . . . but as for Jack, he doesn't notice anything . . . I am worried about the school . . . you know, if he is unmanageable . . ." She also sadly wondered why it was that he had become as he was; was it because he was a boy and the others were girls? "I wonder also if it is because I spoiled him . . . you know I was at home all day . . . I didn't go to work . . . I just stayed with him . . . because the girls were at school . . . and I gave him a lot of attention . . . you know supposing I had gone out to work then I could have said that I gave him no attention and that was the reason . . . but it was not like that . . ."

Throughout this observation Mrs G was deaf to my repeated suggestions that she should seek advice about him at a child guidance clinic nearby. However, by the time she was driving me back to the station she again seemed entirely to deny that Jack had any problem. Yet during the observation, after pouring out her distress, she seemed, at least for a short while, more capable of paying him some attention and Jack seemed able to respond slightly. She told me that Jack liked his books although she immediately added, "Always the same books . . . if you buy new books he tears them up, even at night when he is in bed . . ." She then took one up and showed it to him asking him to repeat the names of the things that he saw. Jack seemed then to come back to life, he even looked less stiff, and he repeated their names quite quickly and distinctly and definitely. A few minutes later Mrs G added, "He knows these books . . . no new books . . . he likes repeating things . . . no new books . . . he doesn't like stories . . . no stories, just repeating . . . but at least he talks . . ." I was quite aware that Jack only liked repeating the same old things just as he liked to live inside his old shell, but at least he was talking which was certainly an advance compared to his complete silence of a few months earlier.

During the succeeding months, up to the time when I finally left, I heard Jack say only a few more words. Otherwise his condition seemed as desperate as before: he spent the whole time curled up on the settee, or wrapped up in the curtain, or hiding in a huge bin. Yet his mother told me that he was beginning to attend a small, local nursery school. His teacher found him to be very disturbed, but after a while he was beginning to improve. He was, as she said, "Still a considerable problem . . . but perhaps a little less unmanageable . . ." Unfortunately I never witnessed his progress. Subsequently, when I wrote to Mrs G from Italy on such occasions as Christmas or Jack's birthday to ask her how Jack and the rest of the family were getting on, I received no answer. So while I still hope that his future may be better than his past, my final and lasting impression of him was that he had become more and more desperately withdrawn.

III

Review

Backwards in time

Since I did not observe these two babies from birth I shall never know how they were right from the start. Martin was already fifteen days old when I saw him properly for the first time, and my first observation of Jack took place around the time when he should have been born had he not been premature; he was then one month old. A fortnight – and even more, a month – is a long time for a baby. Neither had I any means of knowing anything about the nine crucial months of pregnancy. One can only speculate about their life inside the womb. I was, however, in a position to observe the impact that their environment seemed to have on them from very early days and to see some of the means and mechanisms each employed to cope with the impact on them of their post-natal world. Clearly, however, I was not in any position to tell their 'whole' story even over the time when I knew them.

A marked retreat seemed evident in Martin from the beginning: in his closing his eyes to the world, in his obsessive and constant movements, in his resisting novelties and pushing them away with his tongue. Jack seemed to have been born more open although also very vulnerable, and in a sense probably not yet ready to be born. It is impossible to know what kind of influences and experiences they may have felt inside the womb. Yet both babies had come out of the womb at least physically fit for post-natal life and in this respect pre-natal life had proved safe for them. That stage, however, had ended suddenly, and presumably unexpectedly, as their births were traumatic: Martin was born through Caesarean section and Jack was born prematurely. The relative security and protection of the womb was then abruptly replaced by the harsh impact of other human beings and of a world in which they were bombarded by confusion, bewilderment, disappointment, and in Martin's case by humiliation, and in Jack's by absent-mindedness and emotional poverty.

In the narrow world of the womb no harsh sounds are to be heard (remember Martin's extreme sensitivity to sound), nor are cold or hunger felt. Needs are satisfied automatically, probably before being felt. Inside the womb all is enwrapped and safely contained all the time. One may conjecture that experience of the close sustaining support and at-oneness felt by the foetus with the muscular, containing object, the placenta and the amniotic fluid, probably precedes any sense of separation between the containing object and the baby's skin.

Probably in retrospect the wall of the womb feels like a lost safety-barrier or second skin; once its insulation and protection is pierced or removed the baby is left naked and exposed, and dependent upon a receptive external object to protect it and to introduce it to the world and to its own emotionality. Martin and Jack seem to have experienced the transition at birth as a particularly terrifying cataclysm and life outside as a catastrophe or as an assault. Jack, in his frailty, seemed extremely liable to catastrophic experiences of disintegration. Martin seemed to experience everything, including the presence of the nipple inside his mouth, as an assault. One could suppose, in such an event, that life inside the womb might be looked back to in an idealised, nostalgic way. Sooner or later it seemed that both children desperately tried to retreat from the harsh reality of their present and embarked upon a tragic and illusory journey back in time. They tried to ward off people and the outside world while rebuilding around themselves an illusory, bizarre replica of their lost cocoon. In the end Jack spent hours curled up like a foetus, or wrapped, mummy-like, in a curtain. Martin's wish to go back 'in' was clearly evident when he plunged his head into his pillow or, later on, when he tried to push his head against his mother's rounded stomach.

But the womb-like state they tried to achieve had little to do with any real womb, with its components and life-sustaining functions, nor with life inside the womb as a natural and progressive preparation for living in the outside world. Instead it had an anti-life, unnatural and restrictive quality.

Closed inside their 'mental womb' both children were poised towards mental dissolution and death; and this at a time when in the natural course it would have been appropriate for them to open up to a wider world and to a different more psychological containment for their essential selves. Martin and Jack seemed to use all their resources to create some kind of physical, boundary-like barriers to enfold their own naked, probably already injured, nascent selves with, as it were, a tough second skin. At various times this could be a muscular membrane, or a sensory wall or a sensuous coat. For instance, from the very beginning they could be seen continually occupied in constant, rhythmical, rotatory movements. Martin moved his head from side to side or sucked his tongue, moving it round all the time. Jack, when uncontained, usually began by continually moving his arms and legs, then came his head, and then his eyes in a circular kind of movement. At such times they seemed to be building around themselves some kind of protection in a way that reminded me of the movements of a silk-worm spinning its head to make a cocoon. With their obsessive circular motion they seemed to make themselves impermeable and impenetrable to the world around them, their minds being entirely taken up by or focused on their movement or the sensations arising from this movement.

It seemed at times that a similar protective barrier could also be achieved by holding on to some strong sensation; or by creating around themselves a coat of sensuousness when they would attain a kind of trance-like mindless state in which they became almost hypnotized by the sensation of the moment and were thus utterly impenetrable. This could be achieved through sound, or light, or colour, or feeling a texture. However, perhaps the most effective and long-lasting mechanism was masturbation, but less for the excitement deriving from it than for the sensuous pleasure aroused by it. When plunged in one of these orgies Martin seemed entirely to give himself up to the pleasure deriving from it and to be oblivious to the world around him. When holding on to his penis and curled up in the foetal position Jack would seem deaf to everything else and did not even blink if his mother came near him. Sometimes a kind of closure to the outside was also achieved through tension, stillness and stiffness. When thus tense or stiff, Martin and Jack seemed to close every pore, every possible ingress. Jack would also often close his eyes and his lips. With this rigid paralysis they seemed desperately to be trying to paralyse all attacks from the outside or to stop some dreadful event from taking place. I believe that, indeed, almost all events were equally dreaded and were felt as attacks.

Inevitably these pathetic attempts to paralyse both time and the world around them resulted in a paralysis of their own mental development. The artificial membranes they created were entirely defective and leaky, possessing no binding strength and offering neither protection nor containment. Since these were not based on the introjection of some live human object, they had the quality of armour physically keeping them together (vide the extreme attachment they both developed at one point for their coats and how they used to scream with rage or terror if these were removed from them). Wrapped as they were inside impenetrable, non-mental, non-human membranes, Martin and Jack always seemed ready to spill out and to be empty and core-less like some kind of balloon. The inevitable consequence of Jack's series of movements was that he leaked out his milk and would then look completely unbound; he would then begin trembling all over and become progressively blanker and blanker. In the case of Martin sweat would stream from him while he engaged in constant head-shaking or sucking his ever-protruding tongue. But at these times I do not think that Martin and Jack were only losing bodily substances. Nor do I think that their desperate attempts to build some kind of barrier against the painful impact of the world were just wasted effort. They were in fact made at a high cost and were far from harmless. It was as if a butterfly sought to revert to being a chrysalis or larva or caterpillar and so, perforce, had to shed its coloured wings, its legs, antennae and new compound eyes, all in order just to be able to crawl back once more into its old, over-tight cocoon or earlier skin. Likewise Martin and Jack in attempting the costly operation of going 'back in' lost many of the new skills, functions and faculties that they were beginning to acquire after birth. They had also to do violence to all their perceptions in order that they might believe in such an unnatural event. In particular their potential for more mature and complex mental and perceptive operations seemed to have been injured and buried. They appeared to have shed their minds and spent hours in a kind of mindless, blank state. When absorbed thus, they seemed merely to vegetate, their mental life not much more advanced than that of a primitive organism such as a larva or an invertebrate. Jack's eyes were almost always blank-looking no matter what went on around him and no matter what he was doing, whether 'cycling' for hours on end, or shaking the bars of his play-pen, or mechanically hitting his mother's face. Martin too, frequently went completely blank-looking when engaged in his obsessive, constant rhythmical movements. Their blank expression was accompanied by a similar emptiness, dullness and poverty of action, and on a number of occasions I found myself thinking that they very easily could have been mistaken for mental defectives.

Progressively too they each seemed to lose individuality, initiative, personality and character. They both behaved more and more like automata, mechanically repeating the same actions for hours at a time, or else mechanically and unintelligently copying the surface of other people's actions, and later on, of other people's words. In the end they each looked like empty shells, or pathetic shadows who, having lost their identity, just followed others passively, fusing and confusing themselves with anyone who was strong enough to take the lead. In their fusion with whatever was the object of the moment they seemed to live parasitically through it and gave it total power over themselves.

Enclosed within their cocoon Martin and Jack also lost their capacity for expression: Martin almost never cried; Jack too soon gave up crying once he found that his infrequent protests were unheard. Their rare smiles seemed to be so many automatic, indiscriminate, emotionless responses. In the absence of any receptive interested objects to contain their projections, projection as an essential mechanism in mental growth was inhibited. Evacuation through the skin or through different orifices, muscular discharge of tension or escape into flaccidity, seemed to be their most common ways of seeking comfort at a body level.

The power to introject therefore remained grievously impaired. Jack's almost total closure to it manifested itself in such bodily signs as the tight closure of his eyes, of his lips and in his vomiting "all the time". Later it was manifested in his thinness and the frailty of his aspect as in his backwardness. Martin's closure to introjection seemed clear from the start in his attitude to the breast and the nipple which he treated like an intruder to be kept at bay and made harmless through the complicated tongue rituals that he engaged in. Later he would take in concrete, indigestible food in a constant and frantic search to fill some void. His present, near total failure at school bears testimony to his difficulty in learning through introjection rather than by the mimicry that is his own mode.

In their own isolated worlds they seem to need nothing and no one. They appear to have achieved an illusory independence from people and from the requirements of the world, but their independence obviously has the same deceptive quality as has the illusory self-sufficiency and omnipotence of a foetus which cannot know or yet recognize the giving object, but which is still entirely dependent upon it. Any giving object was in fact very quickly discarded or ignored by them before it could leave any trace or before its entry could be felt inside. Martin would imbibe his drink in a split second, almost throwing the liquid into his stomach without experiencing it on the sensitive mucosae of his mouth; thereafter he would quickly throw away the cup or glass. More recently he seems to have resorted to cooking his own food and to stealing from his brothers and friends. Jack too became an expert at stealing food from others without looking at them and ingesting it in a flash while quickly dropping his own plate or cup. Yet at other times Jack and Martin just seemed to absorb things, like a sponge. For instance, they appeared passively to take on completely the characteristics of their environment. In this passive absorption they both seemed to lack any personal filtering or selection system, as if they were still living in a state of fusion with their environment, without proper boundaries or containing skin. In fact I often had the impression that they just wished to be left alone in peace to carry on their illusion of being in a state of fusion, inside the matrix of the womb. Even these womb-like rigid boundaries seemed on occasion to dissolve, and Martin and Jack appeared to be in a condition very similar to some kind of dissolution or near-death, a state of flaccid, immobile, lifeless and blank being. Nothing of this, however, gave any impression of peace; their blank expression could easily change into one of extreme pain whenever there was the smallest awakening of their senses.

Martin, when engaged in his endless controlling rituals, aimed at keeping everything in a state of complete stasis and at such times he certainly did not seem to love life. A positive hatred for life was also present in Jack's behaviour as seen in his attempts to ward off the smallest signs of life by 'blocking off' any movement or sound coming from outside. 'Living proofs' of ongoing life, such as novelties, change and the presence of other people, were resented and 'attacked'. These children's perceptive apparatus, as the provider of such proofs was, therefore, similarly hated, constrained and attacked. Novelties were rapidly blocked off or, instead, nullified by being made part of their own system as seen in the case of Martin when he tried to keep at bay or else to encapsulate the nipple with his tongue. Jack simply avoided looking at people and so his inner world remained empty of them. Martin's interest in people was limited to a few, superficial details, as in his stereotyped, at times bizarre, imitation and echoing of his sister Gloria. Most of the time solitude and the company of the inanimate, static and 'predictable' objects was sought. Both children looked for the known and the foreseen and went over the same old 'things' again and again: Jack, with the same old story books, as his mother said, "No new books . . . the same old story books . . . just repeating . . ."; Martin engaged in his lifeless, endless repetitive games. Neither showed any adventurousness: Jack, when he knew how to crawl, even when put outside his play pen would simply remain there holding on to the bars; Martin, although he walked and ran about almost all the time seemed mainly to be running or 'flying away' from everyone and everything. Each time he pushed his fingers as far as the inside of a drawer he inevitably managed to get them crushed, probably confirming in his mind the danger that any unknown inside had for him. Jack, even when he could talk, refused to exchange even one word with any outside person and remained curled up in the foetal position, blind and deaf to their efforts to establish any sort of communication with him. By the time that I left, his spontaneous speech was limited to a designatory language only, expressing imperious needs like hunger and thirst. Martin, too, avoided any dialogue: he either locked himself away from people (as when he hid in his dark coffin-like cupboard) or else he stuck to them like a shadow or bodily appendage. The prototype for this non-communication was prefigured in the kind of 'non-dialogue' his tongue used to establish with the nipple. When it came to learning to talk, or learning in general, this closure to communication and hostility towards the exploration of anything new became very evident. Martin did indeed develop a verbal facility which at first sight might appear to be quite adequate. However, on looking at this more closely it could easily be noticed that his language very rarely served the purpose of communication, while his learning seemed only to be prompted by the wish to appear to learn. His language was often only an echolalic repetition of what others said, just as his actions were a shadow representation of other people's behaviour. At other times his speech sounded like an accumulation of isolated, unassimilated and often misunderstood words reminding me of his indiscriminate swallowing of enormous amounts of indigestible food. The links between his words were often through juxtaposition of sounds alone, using their 'physical' quality rather than their meaning. His speech therefore often sounded like some kind of word salad composed of disjointed bits of conversation and collections of words with no core or guiding thread. Frequently Martin would use words compulsively to put labels on things; once he had found the right label the captive remained there paralysed and enclosed within its definition, like a mummy within its sarcophagus. His talking and his learning seemed largely designed to ward off communication and to paralyse and control. An example of this can be seen in Observation Two when he built up walls of words while hiding himself behind his book. His collections of words and facts were never allowed to form free, meaningful links internally; they were sealed off from one another, labelled and catalogued, to keep them under control. Possibly he felt that their more lively union might set in motion some uncontrollable idea, some new knowledge which would feel like a dangerous intrusion and a potentially catastrophic event. He seemed terrified of any new knowledge, as if this involved intrusion into his rigid and controlled 'system' which might cause a shattering explosion within his fragile and unprotected self. Later, given his incapacity to let any object in, or to release it and hence to acknowledge either its presence or its absence, it is no wonder that his capacity to form symbols should have been impaired. With his terror of everything outside his illusory cocooning system it is also not surprising that his intelligence and his exploratory capacities should have been diminished together with his power to fantasise, to imagine, to appreciate and to engage in humour. This same impoverishment was obviously even more severe in the case of Jack.

A non-facilitating environment

It may be that neither Martin, nor even Jack, were, in the end, completely crushed and destroyed. Thrown back as they were upon their own primitive resources they appeared more and more to be lost souls living mindlessly and mechanically in a vegetative, primitive state – but at least they were still alive. Had their closure to life and the world been absolute, they probably could not have survived. Some buried hope or initiative seemed to lie dormant within each one of them, just waiting for an appropriate intervention to bring it to life. When Martin's father began to take an interest in him the child began to open up more to the world and to emerge from what, at one time, threatened to grow into some increasingly inhibitory, autistic shell. Jack's sister Katie, and perhaps later his nursery teacher, were able in some degree to pull Jack back from his desperately withdrawn state. All this made me wonder how they might have developed, or even 'blossomed', had their introduction to the world taken place in some other kind of environment.

Martin and Jack, within the microcosm of their families, both encountered an insufficiently facilitating environment; their first contact with people seems to have rendered them fearful of such contact. Both their mothers, for instance, in their different ways, seemed to have been emotionally unreceptive. They were either too far away, too distant or too closed to receive their babies' communications, and at other times seemed too close, too fused and confused with them to make communication possible or, as it were, necessary. Mrs T with her fear of going out, and Mrs G so very 'enclosed', both seemed insulated against receiving infantile distress. But perhaps Mrs T, although remarkably absent-minded and blank, was less insulated from life than was Mrs G, for in her youth she had been able to travel and progress before she retreated back inside her cocoon. Even now, inside her golden walls, she continued to move and to look for some, however illusory, sparkle of life. Though giving birth felt to her like some injury or mortal wound, yet at least it was, or had at some point been felt as, an event, whereas with Mrs G I had the impression that birth had always been a non-event. Jack's birth was never mentioned except to say that it had been premature. She herself had never seemed to have been 'out'; her life was restricted to her house and her most adventurous expeditions went no further than to Brent Cross and Oxford Street. Martin, too, if one compared his state with Jack's almost total closure, was probably able to move a few steps further out into the world and to achieve at least some superficial degree of development, although later this seemed to have come to a standstill.

The satellites of these mother-baby constellations seem also to have been either too close and too little differentiated (notably in Jack's case) or else too invasive and cruel (especially in Martin's case) to give them the security to enable them to explore the different dimensions and new horizons that open up after birth. Both babies seem to have been left alone after birth to move in the open space of the world without there having been any landmark or anchorage or gravitational force to attract them and to bind together their nascent identity. From the beginning Martin was exposed to an indiscriminate bombardment of stimuli, given the almost constant state of excitement and of mindless, aimless movement of the people around him. All these stimuli seemed to have formed a huge, undigested mass inside him with no organizing centre or pole or orientation. Such confused accumulations were unfit to be used for enrichment, as for learning or communication; they caused instead poisoning and confusion (*vide* his pimples and rashes) and he could only discharge them through evacuation (as in his sweating, and later his outpouring of 'word-salads'). All this seemed to have left him starved of meaningful, mental nourishment and of human, substantial objects. In his confusion he kept frantically searching, like an addict, for more and more undigestible food (as seen in his constant eating and later in his obsessive search for exciting friends).

Martin was also exposed to numerous non-casual invasions and to active 'intelligent' attacks which served to render him more and more confused about the qualities of humans and the use that people made of their intellects. These invasions and attacks seemed also to have made him more and more fearful of and impermeable to the outside world and, at the same time, utterly defenceless and easily invaded. As his rigid impermeability was ultimately responsible for his lack of proper individual boundaries he could only repeat the attacks, literally and almost in an unmodified way, upon himself, fusing his identity with the attacker as in his painful orgies of self-stimulation or when shadowing his sister Gloria.

Jack, in contrast, if anything seemed to have been under-exposed. Certainly while his environment was warmer it was a woolly, sensuous kind of warmth only. Most of the time he was just left in a mental void, to more or less hypnotic sleep, or faced with a blank wall. The understimulation he encountered within his environment was probably as incomprehensible and confusing to him as was the bombardment in the case of Martin. Martin's family microcosm was probably too empty of humanity and love while at the same time being too crowded with new painful and incomprehensible sensations and emotions. Conversely Jack's environment was too confusingly similar to that of the womb, but painfully clearly without its benefits. Yet Jack in particular, to begin with at least, seemed to have had a quite clear 'preconception' of what it was that he needed and what it was that attracted him most. His eyes seemed to know what to look for and, whenever they met his mother's they fixated them immediately, stopping their rolling, orbitless motion and a sparkle of life could clearly be seen in them.

But Martin and Jack seldom met their mother's eyes, nor did they seem to have had much access to or space inside their mothers' minds. They were, in a sense, offered 'mere bodies' with no physical holding or sensuous physical contact. This lack of any proper mental holding and of exposure to the mental emotional dimensions of post-natal life seemed to throw these babies into a state of confusion, disintegration, regression, bewilderment. Not having found any adequate 'container' or object which could help them to achieve a harmonious, natural mental development and to bring to full light their as yet insufficiently differentiated or defined nascent self, they resorted to their own bodies and bodily resources to hold themselves together. The absence of any parental caring figure inside them was most apparent. Jack seemed the more deprived, as if he had not had the experience of a parental figure. Martin's world was perhaps more populated but certainly not by many caring people, nor by those who were prepared to treat him in a way appropriate to his age, as his painful orgies testified. In the end he too seemed to be as empty of humane objects as was his younger brother Leo's balloon.

Yet in both families other children could not be said to have developed in anything like a similar fashion even if we allow for their doubtless different natures and circumstances in each case. The two babies here described do seem to have been born with very passive temperaments. Jack, despite his tenacity, seemed incapable of fighting for his needs and gave up without much protest when these were not met. Martin not only seemed to have been born a non-fighter but also evinced great difficulty in opening his eyes and his senses to the world; his tenacity showed only in the obstinacy of his closure to it.

But why it was that Martin and Jack developed in the particular way that they did is a question to which there probably is no complete answer. Simple explanations such as that it was due to their environment, or their mothers, or because of their own natures, or even due to the interrelation of all these factors – though they may all have an element of truth – are too flat and too generic. In this narrative I have tried to some extent at least to take into account some of these varying factors, but I am well aware that there can be no ultimate 'explanation'.

No human being is reducible to simple parameters, and each individual is a unique combination of variants. My tentative answers can only be partial and certainly no general theory could be derived from them. But I hope that through my descriptions certain conclusions will emerge for each reader who may then be able to link them with observations of his own or be stimulated by them to undertake his own direct observation of infants and families, and so add to our total body of knowledge in this complex and infinitely variable field.

Bibliography

Abraham, K.
  Selected Papers. Hogarth Press, 1945

Alvarez, A.
  Two Regenerative Situations in Autism: Reclamation and Becoming a Vertebrate. J. Child Psychotherapy, vol. 6, 1980

Bick, E.
  Infant Observation in Psycho-Analytic Training. Int. J. Psycho-Analysis, vol. 45, 1964
  The Experience of the Skin in Early Object Relations. Int. J. Psycho-Analysis, vol. 49, 1968

Bion, W. R.
  Learning from Experience. Heinemann, 1962
  The Elements of Psycho-Analysis. Heinemann, 1963
  Transformations. Heinemann, 1965
  Second Thoughts. Heinemann, 1967
  Attention and Interpretation. Tavistock Publications, 1970
  Caesura. Imago Editore, 1977

Freud, A.
  The Ego and the Mechanisms of Defence. Hogarth Press, 1937

Freud, S.
  The Interpretation of Dreams. S.E. IV & V, Hogarth Press, 1900
  Introductory Lectures on Psycho-Analysis. S.E. XV, Hogarth Press, 1915–1916
  From the History of an Infantile Neurosis. S.E. XVII, Hogarth Press, 1918
  Group Psychology and the Analysis of the Ego. S.E. XVIII, Hogarth Press, 1921
  Inhibitions, Symptoms and Anxiety. S.E. XXI, Hogarth Press, 1926

Harris, M.
  Thinking about Infants and Young Children. Clunie Press, 1975
  Some Notes on Maternal Containment in 'Good Enough' Mother-
    ing. J. Child Psychotherapy, vol. 4, 1975
  L'apport de l'Observation de l'Interaction Mère-enfant à la For-
    mation du Psychanalyste. Nouvelle Revue de Psych. no. 19, 1979
  Growing Points in Psycho-Analysis Inspired by the Work of
    Melanie Klein. J. Child Psychotherapy, vol. 8, 1982

Joseph, B.
  Persecutory Anxiety in a Four-Year-Old Child. Int. J. Psycho-
    Analysis, vol. XLV, 1965
  The Patient who is Difficult to Reach. Tactics and Techniques in
    Psycho-Analytic Therapy, vol. 2 (P. Giovaccini Ed.), 1975
  Towards the Experience of Psychic Pain. Do I Dare Disturb the
    Universe? A Memorial to W. R. Bion. Caesura Press, 1981

Klein, M.
  On the Importance of Symbol Formation in the Development of
    the Ego. Contributions to Psychoanalysis 1921–1945. Hogarth
    Press. 1930
  Psycho-Analysis of Children. Hogarth Press, 1932
  The Early Development of Conscience in the Child. Contributions
    to Psycho-Analysis 1921–1945. Hogarth Press, 1933
  Notes on Some Schizoid Mechanisms. Developments in Psycho-
    analysis. Hogarth Press, 1946
  On Identification. New Directions in Psycho-Analysis. Tavistock
    Publications, 1950

Mahler, M., Pine, F. & Bergman, A.
  The Psychological Birth of the Human Infant. Hutchinson, 1975

Meltzer, D.
  The Psycho-Analytical Process. Heinemann, 1967
  Sexual States of Mind. Clunie Press, 1973
  The Kleinian Development. Clunie Press, 1979

Meltzer, D. et al.
  Explorations in Autism: a Psycho-Analytical Study. Clunie Press,
    1975
  The Conceptual Distinction between Projective Identification
    (Klein) and Container-Contained (Bion). J. Child
    Psychotherapy, vol. 8, 1982

Rosenfeld, H.
  Psychotic States. A Psycho-Analytical Approach. Hogarth Press,
    1965

Segal, H.
  Notes on Symbol Formation. Int. J. of Psycho-Analysis vol. 38,
    1957
  An Introduction to the Work of Melanie Klein. Basic Books Inc.,
    1973

Tustin, F.
  Autism and Childhood Psychosis. Hogarth Press, 1972

Winnicott, D. W.
  Collected Papers: Through Paediatrics to Psycho-Analysis. Tavis-
    tock Publications, 1949
  The Maturational Processes and the Facilitating Environment.
    Hogarth Press, 1965